"Data is neither mystical nor magical. It is a tool al[ong wi]th... in educators' hands. It can be used fairly or unfa[ir]ly—justly or unjustly, equitably or inequitably. *Equity in Data* shows us how to make ethical, just decisions using data. This is an important book for all educators."

—Dr. Gloria Ladson-Billings, professor emerita, FBA
Department of Curriculum & Instruction, University of Wisconsin-Madison

"*Equity in Data* provides a timely framework for aspiring and current school leaders interested in learning how to make equitable evidence-based decisions. It is a must read for administrative leadership preparation programs and professional development programs for current principals."

—Dr. Travis Bristol, associate professor
University of California, Berkeley School of Education

"*Equity in Data* is a contribution to the literature on how to create equitable classrooms and schools. There's definitely something for everyone here, so add it to your shelves!"

—Elena Aguilar
Author of *Coaching for Equity*

"Collecting, interpreting, and analyzing data can feel daunting to classroom teachers, those whose day-to-day responsibilities are increasingly complex. Not only does *Equity in Data* demystify these processes through the Framework for Equitable Data Culture (EDC), but it also expands our definitions of what counts as necessary data in schools and positions analysis as a collaborative endeavor. Through numerous vignettes from educators, a variety of reflection and application questions, and a myriad of easy-to-engage tools, Knips, Lopez, Savoy, and LaParo have authored a text that is certain to resonate with equity-minded classroom teachers, curriculum specialists, instructional coaches, school administrators, and policymakers alike who seek to actualize student achievement through a justice-oriented lens."

—Dr. Wintre Foxworth-Johnson, assistant professor
University of Virginia's School of Education and Human Development

"The authors provide a much-needed critical framework for centering equity in data use. Rich with practical examples and calls to action, the authors expand our understanding of both the benefits and challenges of using data and how leaders can create an equitable data use culture. They highlight how data use is more than a technical task—it is a way to engage in collective movement toward humanizing and equitable educational practices."

—Dr. Vicki Park, associate professor
San Diego State University's Department of Educational Leadership

"Compelling and brave, *Equity in Data* explores the most important work of an educator: creating equitable opportunities for ALL students to find success. A fearless and comprehensive approach to data selection and analysis, using an equity lens, is essential to this work. This is the guidebook."

—Jenifer Rayne, principal
Pocomoke High School, Maryland

"*Equity in Data* provides critical insight into how to integrate an equity-focused mindset and approach to data analysis in our schools in a manner that interrogates the very definition of data. As school leaders in an inherently inequitable society and educational system, it is our moral obligation and responsibility to disrupt the (in)visible inequitable practices in our schools, but the path to do so is too often unclear. This book provides concrete strategies and resources on how to get that process started.

—Prerna Srivastava, principal
John Welsh Elementary, School District of Philadelphia

"This book was written with such care. From the author descriptions to the data principles, I felt like the information was going to be true, valid, and purposeful. There are few texts that make sure that the reader is comfortable enough to absorb the very important information. This one is special."

—Robyn J. Murphy, MEd, literacy consultant

"*Equity in Data* highlights the importance for school communities to engage in inquisitive exploration. Philly schools, my school included, have benefited working closely with Andrew Knips and his colleagues. Our work together strengthened shared missions through ongoing collaboration in order to threaten inequities in the school system. This book is a clearly written call to action for all who believe in equitable outcomes for our children."

—Heather Martin, teacher
Bayard Taylor Elementary, School District of Philadelphia

"*Equity in Data* beautifully lays out a set of 12 guiding equity principles to help facilitate the journey into how to center equity when making data considerations at the classroom and school level. The authors highlight how it›s not enough to simply view data through an equity lens; they stress the importance of accounting for equity at every step of the data collection process—from planning to analysis to application."

—Michelle Golobish-Gainer, project manager
Office of Diversity, Equity, Inclusion, School District of Philadelphia

"This has the potential to create a real shift in how educators connect to data. It does a masterful job at getting the readier to learn and view the stories of students and teachers/school staff, and the reader is forced to check their own possible biases and privileges along the way. The power of the student testimonies gives readers a doorway into what is really going on every day in the classroom. The School Identity section is something that isn't talked about enough! It is so important to be able to build, review, or analyze data. School identity can unlock so many understandings and bring life and character to data and data-driven processes. Healing-centered engagement should be a fundamental building block for anyone looking to build better school structures and environments for the future."

—Saxon Nelson, director of community engagement
Research for Action in Philadelphia

EQUITY in DATA

EQUITY in DATA

A Framework for What Counts in Schools

ANDREW
KNIPS

SONYA
LOPEZ

MICHAEL
SAVOY

KENDALL
LAPARO

 **ascd** | Arlington, Virginia USA

2800 Shirlington Rd., Suite 1001 • Arlington, VA 22206 USA
Phone: 800-933-2723 or 703-578-9600 • Fax: 703-575-5400
Website: www.ascd.org • Email: member@ascd.org
Author guidelines: www.ascd.org/write

Penny Reinart, *Chief Impact Officer;* Genny Ostertag, *Senior Director, Acquisitions and Editing;* Susan Hills, *Senior Acquisitions Editor;* Julie Houtz, *Director, Book Editing;* Jamie Greene, *Editor;* Thomas Lytle, *Creative Director;* Donald Ely, *Art Director;* Lisa Hill, *Graphic Designer;* Kelly Marshall, *Production Manager;* Christopher Logan, *Senior Production Specialist;* Valerie Younkin, *Senior Production Designer;* Shajuan Martin, *E-Publishing Specialist*

PAPERBACK ISBN: 978-1-4166-3139-2   ASCD product #122021 n10/22
PDF EBOOK ISBN: 978-1-4166-3140-8; see Books in Print for other formats.

Quantity discounts are available: email programteam@ascd.org or call 800-933-2723, ext. 5773, or 703-575-5773. For desk copies, go to www.ascd.org/deskcopy.

Library of Congress Cataloging-in-Publication Data
Names: Knips, Andrew, author. | Savoy, Michael, author. | Lopez, Sonya, author. | LaParo, Kendall, author.
Title: Equity in data : a framework for what counts in schools / Andrew Knips, Michael Savoy, Sonya Lopez, Kendall LaParo.
Description: Arlington, VA : ASCD, [2022] | Includes bibliographical references and index.
Identifiers: LCCN 2022013020 (print) | LCCN 2022013021 (ebook) | ISBN 9781416631392 (paperback) | ISBN 9781416631408 (pdf)
Subjects: LCSH: Educational statistics—Data processing. | Educational equalization. | Education—Methodology.
Classification: LCC LB2846 .K55 2022 (print) | LCC LB2846 (ebook) | DDC 370.72/7—dc23/eng/20220511
LC record available at https://lccn.loc.gov/2022013020
LC ebook record available at https://lccn.loc.gov/2022013021

30 29 28 27 26 25 24 23   1 2 3 4 5 6 7 8 9 10 11 12

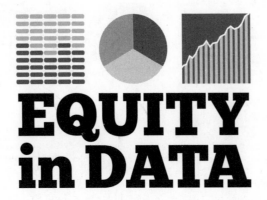

EQUITY in DATA

A Framework for What Counts in Schools

Acknowledgments

The following friends, family, colleagues, experts, and all-around wonderful humans made a lasting imprint on this book. All 68 of them gave their time through interviews, editing, and/or rounds of feedback. They told their stories and shared their expertise, wisdom, and vision. This book is theirs as much as it is ours.

Alana Bouie, Alejandro Gibes-de-Gac, Amelia Coleman-Brown, Anna Younger, Ashley Seak, Betsy Rafferty, Bootsie Battle-Holt, Braheem Watson, Carlye Norton, Carol Cassidy, Chelsea Fay, Christy Chang, Cokettia Rawlerson, Crystal Jameau, Cynthia Chapman, Dan LaSalle, Dan Lopez, Dan Mendoza, David Laver, DeeDee Hendricks, Elin Franzen, Emily Walkiewicz, Erin Mullen, Erina Pearlstein, Farhana Ferdous, Heather Martin, Hezekiah Merchant, Jacqueline I. Hain, Jaimie Foster, Jamie Greene, Jenifer Rayne, Jimmy Kaiser, Karen Drexler, Kaseem Anderson, Dr. Katie Pak, Katie Tedesco, Kelly Aponte, Kim Tim, Kristen Poemer, Laura Boyce, Lauren Thomas, Lenore Franzen, Lindsey Sanborn, Michael Czerniawski, Michael MacArthur, Misty Jewett, Nicole Jackson, Nicole Molino, Dr. Noah Tennant, Noah M. Wager, Patty Kline, Richard Feistman, Roberto Rodriguez, Ryan Scallon, Sade Parham, Sasha Best, Dr. Scott Woods, Sharon Marino, Sofie Vastano, Sophia Seifert, Susan Hills, Susan Raskind, Taylor Uyehara, Dr. Travis Bristol, Vanessa Johnson, Vivek Ramakrishnan, Wintre Johnson, and Zephrah Pam.

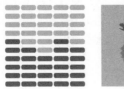

Introduction

Most things that I discuss with you all are not concepts I have mastered but things that I also battle with. We are doing it together.

—Sonya Renee Taylor

Hidden Students, Hidden Data

Malik

"I was a ghost."

Malik—a Black student in a Philadelphia public high school that for years was labeled "persistently dangerous"—hated school. He mostly sat by himself in the corner of his classrooms, in part because his classmates bullied him.

"They always seek out the quiet people," he said. He wanted to fight back, but instead, "I would just cry and run."

For Malik, school also felt like a place with the sole purpose of turning him into an obedient worker. He saw no avenues that would help him achieve his goal of being an artist. He was motivated to study but saw little connection between what he was learning in school and his career aspirations. He wanted high school to look more like college, with the bulk of the curriculum grounded in real-world application. For Malik, school was not about learning—it was about compliance. You play the game, follow certain rules, get your diploma, and then have the baseline credentials to get a job.

Malik liked his teachers in the JROTC and multimedia extracurricular programs, but most teachers didn't know anything about him or his interests, and they certainly didn't know how to engage him in class. "Get the book. Get the pencil. Start writing notes." That was his average experience. He just wanted teachers who showed that they cared, who asked him what his goals were, and who reached out to him personally. He wanted to be challenged.

1

"I would have loved to have read a book that was well above my reading level," he shared. "My teachers saw me as a smart student, and they knew they weren't challenging me." Malik often thought about following in the footsteps of his grandfather, who had dropped out of the same school two generations before because classes were too easy.

* * *

Amy

"I was a complete outcast."

School was a nightmare for Amy, an Asian student in a nationally ranked public high school in New York City. She began hating school in 3rd grade when the bullying began.

"At first, it was racial. But then, because I was quiet, they bullied me more because they knew I didn't stand up for myself." Students called her racial slurs, and Amy had no safe avenue at the school for getting help, so she changed schools. Then she changed schools again … and again.

It never got any better. Along with the bullying came boredom. In her experience, school meant sitting and taking notes she'd forget a few days later. It meant limited opportunities to apply learning to the real world, and it meant isolation.

"I wanted to learn, but I didn't see the point of learning in this kind of environment." Although she cared about her education, Amy would often sleep through lessons, skip class, or take long bathroom breaks. She learned most when she was studying alone at home.

Her senior year, she had 72 absences and was on track to fail. Her teachers intervened every way they could, but "all they cared about was my passing grade because the school needed to maintain their rank. They didn't care enough to help me learn."

As much as Amy loved some of her teachers, most of them let her down. "They made me feel like I was invisible. There were times when my teachers never even bothered looking at me. When I had to present in class, sometimes they would sigh like I didn't even know what I was talking about."

When she saw her grades posted, she internalized them. "I usually had under 65s, and the highest grades I would get were 70s. I felt like such a shitty student—that's just who I am." Her identity as a learner and the view she had of herself were boiled down to a number posted on the wall. Her teachers didn't understand her sense of humor, her passion for music, or her career goals. In short, they didn't know her.

"I wish my teachers would have just come up to me after class to check in and ask, 'How are you feeling about this class?' or 'What's going on in your life?'"

What counts in schools? If you learned that Malik had no disciplinary infractions during his senior year, would you think he had a good experience? If you knew that Amy graduated from one of the top-ranked schools in the country, would you think she learned a lot? Discipline data and graduation rates are important, but they do not usually capture what students want out of their own educational experiences.

Students can often tell which data metrics their schools prioritize. *Use this
Every day, Malik watched his teachers put more energy into enforcing physical compliance in the classroom than providing intellectually challenging work. Amy could see that her teachers were more motivated to help her squeak by with a passing grade than to connect with her emotionally. Both Malik and Amy felt let down by schoolwide data priorities.

There is nothing wrong with prioritizing physical safety when students feel unsafe—as they did in Malik's school. Likewise, there is nothing wrong with helping a student on the cusp of failing, like Amy. However, it is often harmful to lean on systems that chart a problem as a number but neglect that problem as an experience. Malik's school sent a racist message that they would rather control his body than engage his mind. Amy felt like she was just another number the school needed to maintain its rank.

Thankfully, there is an opportunity to realign school data with what students want out of their educational experiences. It begins with baking equity into our data work. When we put equity first, we put students first.

In many schools, equity conversations happen in one place and data conversations happen in another. In your school, do teachers "see every child the same," unaware that they aren't valuing the richness of students' identities and gifts or working hard to confront the biases staff bring to their work? In your professional learning communities, do teacher teams scrutinize a narrow range of student data with little focus on equitable outcomes? In your leadership team meetings, do administrators review the same schoolwide progress reports and then fail to commit to an equitable redistribution of resources? We need to ensure we are using data in service of students—rather than, as we often see, using students in service of data.

Building a better data culture can be the path to greater equity in schools. When we embed equity into our data work, we illuminate disparities, stories, and wisdom that make our schools safer and stronger. We can create an equitable data culture by making five shifts:

1. **Expand our understanding of data** to better identify and use the data we already have at our fingertips. The current, limited definition of *data* limits leaders' ability to capture much of the data that matters.

2. **Strengthen our knowledge of data principles.** Few educators have a background in statistics, but we can learn and apply 12 essential principles as we engage with data in service of equity.

3. **Break through our fear of data** (or, in some cases, our overconfidence in data). Many leaders lean too heavily on premade reports or data protocols that fail to illuminate or address inequities.

4. **Decolonize our data-gathering processes** in favor of more collaboration with the school community. Leaders must move from the mindset of data extraction to a ground-up approach to gathering and using data.

5. **Turn data into meaningful, equitable action.** Too much data never gets used. What comes from data should guide the redistribution of resources in service of equitable opportunities and outcomes.

Throughout this book, you'll encounter principles, tools, and best practices that school leaders can use to create an equitable data culture. The ideas expressed in this book reflect the research, experience, and beliefs of the four coauthors, who are education leaders and practitioners. Much of the book's foundational content stems from our lived experience and more than 40 interviews with school and district leaders, teacher leaders, data experts, and students. The tools and strategies we present have all been field tested (often by ourselves in our own contexts) but have not all been subject to rigorous evaluation. In presenting our work here, we hope readers adapt the relevant tools and strategies to their unique contexts and improve them as they see fit.

Let's begin by defining *data* and *equity* in schools.

Data is humanizing information. Data includes facts and statistics, and in schools, most of those facts and statistics are about people—or how resources, opportunities, and treatment are allocated to people. If we only see data as numbers and outcomes, we severely limit the information we value. Data includes not only assessment scores, graduation rates, and attendance percentages but also people's stories, perspectives, and experiences. A number can't capture the feelings of the only teacher of color on a grade team who is on the verge of quitting. One statistic can't describe the culture of a classroom that's flourishing.

Data includes our informal interactions, like the body language of a teacher during a formal evaluation or the tone of voice a student uses to explain what happened during recess. Most data activates emotions, biases, stereotypes, and biochemical responses, which in turn inform what we say and do. If data is ultimately used to drive our actions in service of equity in schools, then understanding data as more than numbers helps us see the people whom we might otherwise ignore. Expanding the definition of *data* can be a wake-up call to educational leaders who make decisions based on data. When we say data is humanizing information, we also ask those who interpret data to interrogate their own emotions, biases, and experiences.

> **Apply:** *When you think of data, what are your initial thoughts or feelings? How does your definition or understanding compare to the one we use?*

We define *equity* as an umbrella term that refers to fairly distributed resources, opportunities, and treatment that result in comparable outcomes for identity groups. Let's look at each component:

- *Fairly* refers to the absence of favoritism or discrimination, meaning it is just and based on need, such as the treatment of students in a classroom or across a school.
- *Distributed* refers to how those in power exert their power, such as how they allocate school funding, how they assign teaching staff based on need, or with whom they spend their time.
- *Resources* are concrete investments, such as books, money, or time, as well as human resources, such as knowledge of community and child needs or additional teachers and counselors.
- *Opportunities* are the options those in power make available, such as participation in tutoring or access to gifted and talented programs.

- *Treatment* describes the way we engage one another as humans, such as how we speak to certain staff or the attention we give to some students over others in a classroom.
- *Comparable* is the absence of disproportionality, meaning we can't predict outcomes based on a particular characteristic or subgroup.
- *Outcomes* describe markers of success, such as academic performance or graduation rates.
- *Identity* refers to the demographic or sociocultural characteristics society most commonly uses to group people, such as race or gender.

Educational equity, then, refers to fairly distributed resources, opportunities, and treatment *in schools*. Educational equity in classrooms means that teachers distribute resources, opportunities, and treatment in a manner that results in comparable outcomes regardless of identity. School leaders cannot and should not be expected to counteract every oppressive societal force, and they cannot fully redress poverty, housing crises, mass incarceration, or other systemic barriers. Equity will only be realized in society when we take collective efforts across all sectors and industries. Furthermore, equity is not liberation from oppression. Liberation and justice are products of our collective action and much broader than even the most significant education reforms. This book focuses on the actions school leaders can take as they gather and analyze data in service of educational equity. In doing so, we hope to move us a step closer to justice and liberation.

By contrast, *inequity* means that resources, opportunities, and treatment are *unfairly* distributed or result in unequal outcomes along markers of identity. Inequity takes many shapes and forms in our schools and society, and there are some clear causes of inequity, as well as some common explanations that have racist, problematic roots.

Apply: *Can you name concrete examples of how inequity operates in our schools and society? Where does inequity come from, and why does inequity continue to exist in our society? If you don't believe inequity exists or can't articulate why it exists, we encourage you to read the next section thoughtfully or pause here and read our virtual appendices (ascd.org/EquityInDataAppendix.pdf): Quantitative Data Showing Inequity (Appendix A) and Equity and Inequity (Appendix B).*

Explanations for Why Inequity Exists

First, we must acknowledge that schools mirror the many shapes and forms of inequity in our society. Drawing on the research of Glenn Singleton, Ibram X. Kendi, and many others, we share both racist and anti-racist explanations for why inequity exists. We focus on racial inequity, but other lines of difference, such as gender and ability status, could be applied equally.

There are three common racist explanations for why inequity exists:

1. **Genetics or innate differences:** *"I have very good genes."* This argument is the most obviously racist. At its problematic root, this argument falsely suggests that ability is distributed unequally between identity groups (i.e., "Boys are good at _____, whereas girls are good at _____"; "Black people are more _____ than White people"). This is a racist idea that has been perpetuated by European colonists in the 1400s, U.S. presidents from the 1700s to the present day, and researchers such as Charles Murray with his book *The Bell Curve*. Importantly, research has repeatedly debunked all these ideas. The suggestion of genetic differences between racial groups has led to a global history of horrifying acts and the continued oppression of marginalized groups. The result is the castification, segregation, and classification of people by race. Any insinuation that one group is inherently better or more advanced than another group perpetuates arbitrary hierarchies and normalizes inequity.

2. **Poverty or some other variable:** *"It must not be race. It's probably poverty."* Colorblindness often pushes us to seek out other explanations for racial inequity. The argument that race doesn't predict outcomes—but poverty does—is a distraction from the power that race and racism hold. Researchers control for factors such as socioeconomic status when they conduct studies, meaning they examine outcomes between groups that have the same socioeconomic status. Research consistently shows that race plays a statistically significant role. The desire to remove race from the equation reflects a belief in a "post-racial society" where race no longer matters, but that clearly is not our society. This mindset therefore asks marginalized groups to assimilate—to erase their culture and identity in order to fit into the dominant culture.

3. **Culture or choices of the marginalized group:** *"That's just their culture."* This explanation suggests that racial groups choose their outcomes. The common meritocratic and individualistic myth that all people need to do is "pull themselves up by their bootstraps" does not match research around social mobility. It's both a confusing and problematic idea that an entire racial group might simply choose worse outcomes or teach their children to make choices that will hurt themselves.

There are two core antiracist explanations for why inequity exists:

1. **Policies and laws:** Laws, systems, and structures—both current and historical—have created an inequitable society and must be changed or replaced in order to create an equitable society. It's important to note that these policies are not solely in the control of politicians. Schoolwide and classroom policies exist in both racist and antiracist forms. Racist examples include suspension-focused discipline systems or required curricula that only show stereotypical depictions of minoritized groups. Antiracist examples include restorative, healing-centered systems or culturally relevant curricula. The ideas we spread through systems can enact or impede equity by codifying and legalizing how we collectively operate.

2. **Culture or choices of the marginalizing group:** Humans are policymakers in the spaces where they yield power, great or small. What we say and do, even on the smallest level, matters. Where we spend our money, when we are silent or speak up, whom we shame and love—all our actions move us further from or closer to equity. This does not mean that everyone has equal power, but it does place the ownership for enacting equity on those with power—not on the people who are being oppressed. Protests from marginalized groups are an example of collective empowerment. However, without a shift in the behaviors—not just mindsets—of the marginalizing group, there will be little meaningful progress toward equity.

Book Organization and Terminology

This book is intended to be a broad resource for improving equitable data practices throughout the school. Therefore, we've structured the book to introduce principles and frameworks in the first two chapters that are then applied to different facets of school leadership in the rest of the book. We believe inequity must be tackled in *all* parts of a system and that building an equitable data culture in just one part of the school is not enough.

As you read, you'll encounter insets between chapters. One describes a set of 12 data principles, and a second describes common data meeting "traps." Chapter 1 presents the core of the book: a framework for an equitable data culture (EDC). Chapters 2–8 apply EDC and the data principles to different domains of the school. Chapter 2 describes high-level data practices, including two forms of equity audits and guidance around equitable goal setting. Chapter 3 presents the "gifted lens" for gathering classroom data and includes a model of how to talk with students about their academic data. Chapter 4 applies "healing-centered engagement" and restorative practices to improving student well-being. It also presents informal approaches to gathering data about students and a critical incidents tracker to replace traditional disciplinary processes.

The book then shifts to supporting teachers. Chapter 5 describes recruiting, hiring, and evaluation best practices. Chapter 6 provides a detailed walkthrough of EDC using an example of a professional learning community. Chapter 7 examines two approaches to professional learning that center both data and equity: action research and coaching. Finally, Chapter 8 concludes the book by highlighting its big ideas and making a call to action.

Throughout the book, we include icons in the margins that call attention to where data principles (DP) and EDC show up.

Our choice of language in this book is intentional. The terms we use are meant to reflect respectful nomenclature at the time of publication, but our language is constantly changing, so more frequently updated sources will have up-to-date guidance. We also understand that some readers will not agree with the terms we use. We include a brief explanation of our language choices in the following section, but we want to emphasize they may not resonate for every person.

Terms Related to Race, Gender, and Sexuality

- **People of color:** "The term 'people of color' was a phrase chosen by Black, Latino, Native American, and Asian and Pacific Islander activists in the 90s to actively decenter whiteness" (Plaid

& MacDonald-Dennis, 2021, para. 5). We honor that language and recognize that the term is already meant to be inclusive of racial groups of color. People of color are not a monolith, and there are differences within and across racial groups and ethnicities.

- **Black, White:** There is widespread disagreement about when to capitalize racial terms. In some literature, Black is capitalized and "white" is not. There are strong arguments on both sides (Ewing, 2020; Yang, 2020). We capitalize all racial terms both for consistency and to acknowledge the meaning they hold as both social constructs and systemically reinforced categories.
- **They/them pronouns:** We include a lot of examples in this book. In support of nonbinary people, we generally default to using they/them pronouns in order to remove unnecessarily gendered language. We similarly avoid phrases such as *boys and girls* and use the term *Latinx* to be inclusive of all genders.
- **LGBTQIA+:** We use this term (rather than LGBT) to be inclusive of a wider—although not comprehensive—range of gender identities and sexual orientations.

Humans are beautiful, unique, multifaceted individuals with intersectional identities, and we recognize that our terminology lumps together some identities and leaves out others. However, we chose language we hope shows respect for intersectional identities and conveys the power of data in working for equity.

Additional Terminology

The word *data* is technically plural. In this book, though, we defer to the informal use of *data* as a singular noun to enhance readability.

There are two distinct gaps in education that are often conflated: opportunity gaps and achievement gaps. The former describes access, whereas the latter describes outcomes. Opportunity gaps and achievement gaps work in tandem; if you have less access to opportunities, then your outcomes won't be as good. Data work must therefore focus on understanding both opportunity and achievement, remembering that achievement is often a construct defined by those in power and measured against metrics that are biased and inequitable (Kendi, 2019). Gloria Ladson-Billings adds a third powerful term, *education debt*, which addresses the "historic, economic, sociopolitical, and moral foundations of the disparate education outcomes between white students and students of color" (Alliance to Reclaim Our Schools, 2018). Eula Biss similarly writes of *White debt* and the need for White folks to repair harm (Biss, 2015). The word *debt* helps us move ownership to people in power and shift our attention to reforming the policies that shape our education system—as opposed to reforming the students who operate within that system.

We often hear the term *under-resourced* when describing students and families in communities of color. Our school system values resources historically limited to White families, such as money, advanced college degrees, and volunteer hours from families who have the luxury to take time off work. Conversely, our school system typically devalues resources from people of color, such as knowledge of community and child needs, cultural practices, and perspectives on injustice. Impoverished communities are often resource-rich; they are just not financially rich. We prefer terms such as *access*, *funding*, *capital*, *money*, *power*, *political influence*, and *institutional knowledge* to refer to the specific types of resources that prevent or perpetuate education debt.

Coauthor Statements

As coauthors, we refer to ourselves as *we* throughout this book to reflect the collaborative nature of our work and the book. In some instances, we describe our individual experiences and use our individual names in the third person (e.g., Sonya). We each carry unique power, biases, experiences, identities, and lenses. The following sections are our personal statements about what brings us to this work.

Andrew Knips, The Imposter

I wrote this book from a lens steeped in privilege, wealth, masculinity, and Whiteness. I feel like both an elitist and an imposter—someone with power and access who is simultaneously unaware and inexperienced. There is so much I don't know about data, education, and equity, in part because I carry my "White racial frame" (Feagin, 2013) with me wherever I go. I walk this world with nearly every privileged identity, and I believe it's time for people like me—in collaboration with people who are not like me—to take more action and risks.

Honest self-examination should lead to the conclusion that all educators feel like imposters in some shape or form. Novice teachers feel it when they rewrite the previous year's frantically assembled lesson plans. Veteran teachers feel it when they grow detached from an increasingly younger generation of children. A teacher with a hidden disability might feel like an imposter during a staff team-building activity in which they aren't comfortable participating. New school leaders feel it when they suddenly step out of the classroom and realize that leadership is not as easy as it looks. Veteran school leaders feel it when they are faced with the same "new" district initiative from a decade earlier. Indeed, a White principal might feel like an imposter at back-to-school night while speaking with mostly families of color.

We all feel like imposters in education because our field is an inequitable place and the path forward is murky at best. In my dozen years working in schools, I have yet to find any clear answers. Learning is an unfathomably underfunded science, with pedagogy rooted in outdated practices and unable to keep pace with a changing society. We talk of 21st-century learning, even though we're almost one-quarter of the way through and have limited information about what our society will look like in even a decade, and we still know only a fraction of what there is to know about how the brain works. Education is one of the most basic and complex human experiences we have yet to understand.

Ten years after my dad died, I finally started seeing a therapist. In therapy, I quickly realized that I spend far more time in my head than in my heart. I default to writing, researching, intellectualizing, judging, and analyzing—ubiquitously agreed-on best practices when it comes to engaging with data. It takes extra labor and intentionality for me to break from that tendency and focus on my feelings. However, when I do, I'm happier. I'm more flexible, fun, and empathetic. I'm a better listener. I pay closer attention to "street data" (Safir & Dugan, 2021), which is data from students and families. I'm better able to focus on other people and their needs. To me, this book reflects the value of the heart as we engage in data work. We all feel less like imposters when we see that none of us has the answers; rather, *all of us* have the answers.

Bobbie Harro (2000) describes "waking up" as a key stage in the process of liberation from socialization. Waking up is an internal change about what a person believes about themselves. It took me 25 years to realize I have always been unencumbered because of my privilege.

Waking up is now a daily experience for me. One of those awakenings was during an interview for this book with an assistant superintendent who wondered why I wasn't writing the book with other people, specifically people with different identities. I had no answer. Two months later, I began working with three incredible coauthors who each brought diverse identities and an expanded perspective to the weak rough draft I had assembled on my own. They had an immediate impact on the book, and my solo journey of being the imposter transitioned into a coalition of brilliant people and powerful perspectives.

I still bring my biases to the book, but coauthorship has highlighted the power of collaboration in creating accountability for bias. Coalition building has helped me break away from default characteristics of White supremacy culture—individualism, urgency, and perfectionism—that limit my potential and that of others. Collaboration has also helped me make my daily climb up Tema Okun's ladder of empowerment (2006), constantly aspiring to antiracism in my choices and interactions. I am grateful to my coauthors; the dozens of people we interviewed; family members, friends, and professionals who edited and reviewed drafts; and the litany of researchers and experts who provided the foundation for this book.

We do this work the same way we walk this world: together.

Sonya Lopez, The Data Poet

Growing up, I never felt at home within any single data point—particularly when it came to my identity. "Your last name is Lopez? Do you speak Spanish?" "No way, you're Chinese? I don't see it." "No way, you're Puerto Rican? Why do you talk like you're White?" "Wow, your dad's afro!" "Oh, your mom's English is great." "You're an exotic mix." "You're a mutt."

There are countless studies and stories that raise similar experiences of identity. There is privilege and power, as well as grief and loss. Although it was at times overwhelming, sometimes all I could hear was "not enough."

My own self-concept and sense of identity evolved, but I continued to feel the world around me glitch while processing me as a data point. I did not fit into the provided conventions. I wasn't Cantonese enough here; I wasn't Boriqua enough there. I was at once not relatable and too relatable, approachable and threatening. When I was younger, survival meant striving to be a better data point. Throughout various milestones in my life—first-generation college student, graduate school, employment, coauthoring this book—this internalized misunderstanding crept back in. Thankfully, I've continued the work of healing from it—becoming an athletic collector and user of data. Of course, it took time for me to see it this way. I just thought I loved people and enjoyed studying our minds, habits, and healing. As a result, I was drawn to learning about identity, relationships, and everything in between.

For me, there was no better (or more fun) way to understand these concepts than through the eyes of kids. From kindergarten all the way up, kids are impressively cool people and deserve reminders that they don't need to "be better data points," even when the systems or people around them seem to demand this. In fact, they deserve better systems. This belief became my path to teaching and social work.

In my work, I often reflect on the balance between understanding and change. In most schools, this balance is centered on data and how we use it. To an ELA teacher at heart, this can feel like wrestling with the grammatical comforts of prose and the refreshing thrills of poetry. Data and grammar follow a similar, predictable arc. Learn the rules (all of them), study the systems and structures, practice the mechanics, and construct a meaningful (within the rules) story. In poetry, though, an eye for grammar simply allows us to see when rules are broken. We're invited to see how sentences, words, and sounds behave differently when conventions are dismantled. What was once a defect is now defection. The power in defying the status quo can become a part of a poem's purpose and impact. Poetry offers an opportunity to frame grammatical analysis as a potential exercise of power, not conformity. To me, this book is an endeavor to pursue the poetic forms of data analysis.

In theory, conventions in data or grammar maximize the clarity and soundness of information. In practice, these conventions can dictate what, or whom, will be seen or heard. Grammar has been, and continues to be, exacted as a tool of White supremacy—from policing ideas to propping up barriers for entry. Unfortunately, we've seen data and data analysis yielded to perpetrate strikingly similar harms.

"Tell a story with your data." We hear this a lot in education. I hope this book helps you practice poetically with data and hold space for the poetry of classrooms, hallways, and neighborhoods. As school leaders and educators, it is our professional responsibility to approach data in this way. Audre Lorde (1984) reminds us, "Poetry is not a luxury. It forms the quality of the light within which we predicate our hopes and dreams toward survival and change, first made into language, then into idea, then into more tangible action" (p. 37).

Michael Savoy, The Noise Maker

They say the data speaks for itself, but what does that mean for the outliers we don't understand? Well, we tend to ignore those. They're outside the norm. Not helpful. Noise. If that's the case, then I am "noise," and that is what drives me in this work and the reason I wanted to work on this book. I grew up in a rural part of an East Coast state. My family ended up there because my parents, who were the first in both their families to go to college (my father is the second youngest of 14 siblings, so that's big noise), met at the historically Black college down the street. It was one of the only colleges that welcomed Black students—the so-called noise of society—and it was where they felt wanted. My father became the first Black administrator at one of the local high schools and led the school for 15 years, a tenure unheard of these days. We were the only Black family in our Catholic church (spiritual noise), and because both my parents were educators, I was the only Black male in my core "smart kid" classes by the time I hit middle school (classroom noise). I've been the noise most of my life, in both professional and social circles.

As the living embodiment of noise, I look for other noises around me. What and who are most other people overlooking? How do I help those situations and people become loud enough noise to get noticed and understood—to matter?

I remember one moment as a math coach, sitting in an elementary school classroom in upstate New York, when a teacher called on students to explain their solutions to math problems. A young Black male, seemingly the noise in his classroom, explained how he solved a problem. It was unique. It was different from how anyone else in the room solved the problem, and according to the teacher, it was wrong—not because it was inaccurate or invalid when one took time to really look at it but because it was too "noisy." The teacher couldn't be bothered with noise. My heart hurt that day. I knew how that student felt. He too would either embrace being noisy or, like too many, become silent. He'd be filtered out.

I do this equity work because I do not want anyone to feel like they are just noise. I encourage everyone to listen to and appreciate the noise. We need to discover what's special about the noise and learn from it. I hope this book helps us do that.

Kendall LaParo, The Data "Expert"

I fell in love with data analysis as a 5th grade teacher in Camden, New Jersey. This was quite the surprise to me as someone who had not once opened a spreadsheet and who had flitted between the music school and English department throughout college. I was someone who valued creativity, art, and the human experience—not cold numbers, boring spreadsheets, and inscrutable data tables. I was a people person, and I wanted to help people, not move numbers from one cell to another. Nevertheless, becoming a teacher helped me see data in a new way. Data became a tool. Sometimes, that tool could be used for evil, but it could also be used to enlighten, support, and *help* people.

I began to love making trackers for my classroom and engaging in "practitioner research," in which I planned improvements to my teaching and evaluated my successes using student data. The more interested I became in practitioner research, the more interested I became in the education research happening outside my classroom. I was particularly preoccupied by research on the societal forces—racism and poverty—that kept rearing their ugly heads inside my classroom. I could see the symptoms of systemic racism and intergenerational poverty play out in the lives of our best and brightest children, and I felt relatively powerless as a teacher to do much about it.

I decided to leave teaching to pursue a PhD in sociology with a concentration in race and ethnicity. The idea was that I would pursue research full-time and answer some of my big questions about why the world is organized the way it is—which is to say, deeply unfairly. I learned a ton in graduate school, but the more classes I took, the more I realized that many of my 5th grade students knew more about racism at the age of 10 than I, a White woman, ever would in my whole life, no matter how many books I read.

It became clear that the definition of *expert* in our society is deeply flawed, perhaps even inverted. Today, I am a full-time quantitative researcher and continue to work in education. I absolutely love my work and, although I still haven't found any neat and tidy answers to my big questions, I feel like I can devote every day to pursuing more equitable education systems. I am now on a mission to make both data analysis and equity work more accessible to those who feel that either pursuit is "not for them."

As a data analyst, I believe part of my work is helping others find patterns that bring inequities to light, light fires of action in educators, and make the impact of systemic racism undeniable. Too often, educators—especially White educators such as myself—misidentify academic outcomes and opportunities, mislabel causes and effects, and miss out on patterns of injustice that we ourselves perpetuate. We respond to test data with misplaced interventions in the absence of systemic and structural changes to our systems, schools, and classrooms. We allow data analysis to trick us into thinking we are doing the work, instead of recognizing that we are soothing our own guilt with misplaced efforts that reinforce racist narratives.

Many equity advocates emphasize that equity work is hard work, and they ask that folks "put in the work" and "do their research"—sentiments with which I completely agree. Especially for White people such as myself, it takes a massive amount of unlearning and humility to reverse the racist messaging in which we've been steeped and to find our footing toward antiracist messaging. I would also add that we need to find ways to make this hard work more accessible to everyone. Just as racism is now in the water, soil, and language around us, we must weave antiracism into the fabric of our society. I believe there is a world in which antiracism can be just as prevalent—a world where people just have to reach out and grab it.

Learning from a Pandemic

The COVID-19 pandemic irrevocably altered the American conception of education. Never before had we marshalled so many resources at a moment's notice to redistribute unheard-of and much-awaited support to those our system had ignored for decades. In just a few months, we put laptops in nearly every home, expanded internet access, and dramatically shifted our approach to teaching.

Nevertheless, many still suffered during the pandemic. Kindergartners missed out on the school playground. First graders who were struggling with reading lost access to physical copies of books and high-impact small-group instruction. High schoolers who were on the cusp of dropping out stopped attending school. College students who were working to pay for tuition lost their jobs. Teachers with their own school-age children juggled teaching and parenting. Countless people lost loved ones.

Our schools' rushed, scrappy solutions provided an insufficient bandage for an already damaged and underfunded system. Still, our response to the pandemic taught us how swiftly and radically we can redistribute resources and overhaul school policies when we decide there is an emergency.

Eliminating educational inequity is a similar situation. We all need to come together. We need a massive financial investment. We need to listen to the people we claim to serve. And we need to change the data culture in our schools. Now is the time to look beyond traditional metrics and break from our obsession with numbers and data practices that oppress people. Humanizing our schools can be education's vaccine, and together we can be the experts who discover it.

The Colorblind Backlash

In 2020, in the midst of the pandemic, the Black Lives Matter movement and other activists sparked a racial reckoning in U.S. schools in the wake of Derek Chauvin's murder of George Floyd. White folks throughout the United States—many for the first time—confronted their privilege and learned about systemic racism. Teachers who had previously not talked about race in their classrooms started planning lessons about racial justice. School and district leaders initiated implicit bias training and added words such as *equity* and *liberation* to their vision statements. For the first time in decades, it felt like a collective force was making antiracism a priority.

Then, predictably, pundits and politicians responded with a racist counternarrative. They framed critical race theory (CRT), which has been a branch of legal scholarship about systemic racism since the 1970s, as a threat to schools and an attack on American values. They challenged antiracism with colorblindness, confusing *talking about* racism with *being* racist. At the time of writing, efforts were underway in 36 states to restrict education about race, bias, and racism under the umbrella label of CRT (Stout & Wilburn, 2022).

This manufactured backlash against acknowledging race and racism is not the first challenge to antiracist work in schools, and it will not be the last. Antiracism in schools is essential, lifelong work. We now have an opportunity to resist this colorblind backlash. We can and must examine race and other identities when we consider what data will guide our work. We must persist through the threats and challenges if we want to achieve educational equity.

This is the context in which this book was written and published: a global pandemic and ongoing overt racism. Before you continue, take a moment to feel the weight of these challenges and the opportunities in front of us. Consider your responsibility as a leader to fearlessly forge ahead, innovating, inspiring, and transforming education.

Eight virtual appendixes with supplementary
content are available to download here:

ascd.org/EquityInDataAppendix.pdf

Equitable Data Principles

The following equitable data principles guide leaders as they plan for data collection, engage in data analysis, and make plans based on data. These principles complement the framework you'll encounter in Chapter 1.

Principle 1: Follow Research Ethics **DP1**

Participants benefit from ethical data and research practices. The Belmont Report (Office for Human Research Protections, 2018), a foundational publication that defines *ethical research*, lays out three basic ethical principles that can be applied to data in schools: respect for persons, beneficence, and justice. Respect the people who are giving you their data (typically students) as research participants. Minimize any burden (such as lost class time) that comes with the research. Make sure students directly benefit from what you learn.

Principle 2: Data Is Fluid **DP2**

Data categories are made up but still important. It might surprise you to know that there is no universal, or even national (in the United States), definition of what it means to read on grade level. Every assessment publisher and school district can set a different definition of grade-level reading proficiency. This means that one student can be both below and above grade level *at the same time*, depending on the assessment. Although it is important to have a sense of student performance and growth, keep in mind that assessments create arbitrary cutoffs for proficiency and do not represent an objective truth.

DP3 ⬛ Principle 3: Garbage In, Garbage Out

Your conclusions are only as good as your raw data. It is a waste of time to analyze the data from a vaguely written exit ticket or an incorrectly administered assessment, yet it happens all the time in schools. Strong, accurate, and user-focused data is the bedrock of data analysis. If you do not believe in the accuracy of the raw data, then you should not move on to the analysis phase.

DP4 ⬛ Principle 4: Speed and Accuracy Should Be Balanced

If you want data quickly, you risk inaccuracy. If you want data to be accurate, it's going to take more time. This is true for every step of the process—from planning to gathering to analysis. Think carefully about your data collection needs to strike the right balance between speed and accuracy. The data that school leaders use often comes from busy teachers who have a lot of priorities other than perfect data entry. For teachers, a quick multiple-choice exit ticket saves time, but it may not provide a particularly accurate picture of student learning. You have a much better sense of whether a student understands a math concept if they explain their thinking in a word problem than if they complete a multiple-choice question they have a 25 percent chance of guessing correctly. This doesn't mean that speedy data is useless, but it does mean you should carefully consider the tradeoff. Leaders should gather both slow and fast data, depending on how critical it is to their work.

DP5 ⬛ Principle 5: Data Is Everywhere

"Mixed methods" and storytelling include valuable data beyond datasets. If there's one thing to take away from this book, it's that the concept of *data* includes more than just numbers. It's all around us; it's the outcomes and the emotions, the trends and the outliers, the groups and the individuals. Whatever data you examine, remember that you're only getting a slice of reality. Mixed methods research, in which you analyze both quantitative and qualitative data, is the best way to understand what is going on in a school.

Derrick Bell, the father of critical race theory, said, "Statistics cannot… begin to express the havoc caused by joblessness and poverty" (Bell, 2018, p. 4). When numbers fall short of capturing the full picture, storytelling steps in. One assistant superintendent described how student stories can help us engage in equity work: "When you start to talk to students and follow them, you get experience in what they are experiencing. And you see how their experiences often break down along racial lines."

Principle 6: Keep It Simple

Good data analysis doesn't need to be sophisticated. Most teachers and principals don't have a background in multivariate statistics, and that's OK. There's no need to conduct a sophisticated analysis every time. A teacher might send a text to families asking, "On a scale of 1 (not at all) to 5 (a lot), how much does your child enjoy reading?" Then the teacher might follow up with the four families that responded with the lowest scores. In other words, the teacher doesn't need to know that the average score was a 4.3 with a standard deviation of 0.2.

Principle 7: Analyze Trends *and* Outliers

The trends hide the extremes, and the extremes don't reflect the trends. If we only look at the averages, then we miss the individuals. A student who fails a test that the rest of the class did well on still deserves attention and follow-up work. However, trends are useful because they either confirm or contradict our assumptions about how we are doing overall. It's easy to fixate on the students performing the worst and lose the larger picture that most students are on track. Trends help us understand if what we are doing is working, whereas extremes help us understand who needs extra support.

Principle 8: Disaggregation Reveals Inequities

Data is best understood when broken into subgroups, including race and gender. Disaggregating numbers means separating data into smaller pieces, or subgroups. The federal government breaks down academic and discipline data by race, gender, and disability status for every school, but leaders are often hesitant to do the same within their own schools and classrooms, even though classrooms are the building blocks for the national data. We often prefer to disaggregate data by more comfortable markers, such as standard, grade, or teacher—as opposed to markers that generate more powerful conversations around inequity. Put simply, we won't see the racial impact of policies if we don't examine and talk about racial outcomes at the most granular level.

Kimberlé Crenshaw coined the term *intersectionality* in 1989 to highlight the intersection of multiple identities. For instance, if you are a wealthy Latina woman, you don't necessarily understand what Latino men in poverty experience. Equitable data practices often require us to layer together or detach (control for, in statistical terms) subgroups from one another to better understand dynamics. When we illuminate inequities between and within subgroups, we elevate individual experiences. We can begin to understand how White students experience school, how White female students experience school, and how White female LGBTQIA+ students experience school. Each layer of disaggregation and intersectionality helps us home in on what's happening within smaller subsets of the population.

DP9 ⬛ Principle 9: Apples ≠ Oranges

Don't compare 2nd grade to 3rd grade or biology to chemistry. At a professional development session for teachers, the facilitator showed a chart to the group and asked, "Why do we see a significant dip in reading scores across the district from 2nd grade to 3rd grade?" The problem wasn't that students were necessarily doing worse in 3rd grade; it's that the assessment students take in 3rd grade is completely different from the one they take in 2nd grade. We don't know if kids are suddenly underperforming or if the test just got disproportionately harder. Similarly, some leaders might become concerned when they see that a biology class scored worse than a chemistry class. It is surprisingly common to make unhelpful comparisons such as these. Instead, compare the school or classroom's scores to the state average or to your school's goal. Another approach is to examine the performance of a single cohort of students over the course of the year or from year to year, which is what researchers call a longitudinal study.

Principle 10: Triangulation Adds Credibility DP10

Critical friends and triangulation help validate your conclusions. Data analysis should not be done alone. We need teams, colleagues, and a network of critical friends examining data collectively if we want to combat confirmation bias. Even examining data with a team of diverse colleagues can't eliminate all bias, which is where external validity comes in. External partners, communities of practice, and external evaluators help provide a less biased perspective. Triangulation means gathering data in more than one way on the same topic. Maybe you're holding focus groups after giving a survey. Maybe you notice a concerning pattern in data that shows kids skipping class, so you spend some extra time monitoring the hallways. Maybe the instructional coach tells you there are two 4th grade teachers who are really struggling, so you follow up with the dean to get their input. We ask teachers to use triangulation whenever we expect them to use multiple assignments to determine a student's marking period grade.

Principle 11: Data Gives Clues, Not Answers DP11

Data is the temperature, not the diagnosis. Data won't tell us everything we need to know to fix a problem. Data is the beginning of the conversation, not the end. We so badly want a data point or dataset to give us the answer, but they instead spark more questions—and that's how it should be. Learning that student attendance dropped from 94 to 85 percent between February and March gives us an important data point, but it doesn't illuminate *why* attendance dropped or *what* to do about it. As you consider actions to take for equity, it's your job to use clues within the data to diagnose problems and brainstorm solutions.

Principle 12: The End Users Know Best DP12

Teachers deserve data tools that are helpful and easy to use. Who is ultimately going to see and use the data? If you haven't already, ask teachers how they gather data in their classrooms. Finding out what backup systems they are already using will help you understand their needs. For instance, some teachers use ClassDojo, not because it's required but because it's user-friendly. Many teachers design their own data collection tools to track student attendance, participation, well-being, and achievement. Their systems—whether they use spreadsheets or sticky notes—are often just as, if not more, valid than formal systems required across the school or district. Teachers are almost always going to be the end users, the actual practitioners who best know what will be used and what will be ignored.

1

A Framework for Equitable Data Culture

Not everything that can be counted counts,
and not everything that counts can be counted.

—Albert Einstein

Data Scaredy Cats and Data Warriors

It was the week before the start of the new school year and Andrew was preparing for the professional development session he would be facilitating about data analysis. While reflecting on the school leaders who would attend the session—and their feelings about data—he knew he'd likely encounter two types of data leaders: the data scaredy cat and the data warrior.

Data scaredy cats might be heard saying, "I'm bad at data analysis." They might even have a visceral negative reaction to the word *data*. Many believe data analysis is a secret formula that requires intensive technical training. If there are insights hiding somewhere deep within the school databases, data scaredy cats aren't sure how to find them.

By contrast, data warriors have leaned in, hard, to data analysis in schools. They run regular data analysis meetings and aren't afraid to dive into spreadsheets of raw assessment scores or a student work analysis session. They might sometimes feel frustrated at the lack of visible progress that data analysis has had in their school, but they are proud of the "aha" moments and concrete improvements that have come out of their data analysis initiatives.

After kicking off the professional development session, Andrew sent participants into small groups to discuss the following two questions:

- When you hear the words *data analysis*, what feelings come up?
- When you analyze data, what steps do you usually take?

> Participants then shared in the full group. Not surprisingly, the data scaredy cats (80 percent of the group) named feelings such as anxious, frustrated, and confused, whereas data warriors (the remaining 20 percent) had reactions such as excited, happy, and helpful.
>
> When the discussion turned to the steps of data analysis, answers were varied. Some participants were stuck, and others used the steps from a data analysis protocol with which they were familiar.
>
> *Importantly, Andrew noticed that none of the participants mentioned anything about equity.*

Most educators do not incorporate equity into their understanding of data. Similarly, most data protocols leave out equity. In the previous anecdote, Andrew's training helped demystify the conceptual core of data analysis and highlight equity's necessary inclusion in that work. Grounded in his observations of thousands of leadership team and teacher meetings, Andrew developed the BITES framework, which can be applied to virtually any set of data, whether it be qualitative or quantitative; academic or behavioral; schoolwide, class-level, or individual.

Here is the framework Andrew shared with the group:

- **B:** Bar
- **I:** Individuals
- **T:** Trends
- **E:** Equity
- **S:** Steps

B (Bar) refers to the target against which you will measure your data. It is what you'll ideally encounter, such as student mastery of an objective or the school meeting its goal. When setting the bar, you might review an exemplar response to clarify the grade-level expectation of an assessment. You might examine the walkthrough "look-fors" before observing a teacher. You might remind yourself of the school attendance goal before reviewing a report on the week's attendance average. When we review the bar, we set a clear expectation for what we hope to encounter in the data *before* we look at the data. Engaging in norming activities and having standards, rubrics, and exemplars make this stage easier.

I (Individuals) refers to individual results or data points you will compare to the bar. You focus on what's happening on a granular level—both strengths and growth areas. In this stage, you might notice that six students wrote essays that met all the criteria on the rubric. You might identify three students who had the most negative responses on the first-day-of-school survey. You might make a list of the students with the lowest attendance. During this (and the next) stage, you make observations without drawing conclusions or setting next steps.

If you're looking at a large dataset, you might feel tempted to skip this stage and focus only on trends rather than individual students, but large datasets are where individual narratives and needs often get lost. Humans with real stories are often marginalized when we call them "outliers" or when they are treated like "noise," as Michael described in the Introduction. In some cases, your data analysis will be of a single teacher or student. In those cases, the I and T stages are functionally the same.

T (Trends) means you look for patterns—positive, negative, and surprising—across the data and compare them to the bar. What do you notice? What don't you notice? What is repeated? In this stage, you might discover that most 2nd graders struggled with the final /s/ sound. You might notice that half of all 9th graders understood the concept of a linear equation but made computation mistakes. You might realize that 72 percent of all disciplinary incidents from the previous week were instances of student–teacher conflict.

Having your data ready to disaggregate by subgroup will make pulling out trends that specifically show inequity much easier. For example, noticing that attendance is 4 percent above the goal is helpful, but it might be even more helpful to know that attendance for students with IEPs is 2 percent *below* the goal. The overall trends tell you the average story; the subgroup analyses tell you where to focus your energy.

E (Equity) prompts you to intentionally pause and discuss equity—or, more accurately, inequity—in the data. You'll draw out inequities by disaggregating the data by identity markers. Are Black students doing better than Latinx students? Are boys doing better than girls? Are students without IEPs outperforming students with IEPs? Do English language learners (ELLs) have a stronger grasp on the concept than native English speakers? Identifying what inequities are playing out is key as you begin to determine next steps. We can't have equitable classrooms, opportunities, or results if we don't take time to talk specifically about the implications of disaggregated data. Often, it is difficult to look at outcomes based on identity, in part because as a society, we've confused *talking* about identity with *prejudice* about identity.

S (Steps) refers to the next steps you'll take. You clarify concrete and specific action steps around how you will reallocate resources to address challenges the data illuminated. This stage should be a direct response to what you discovered in the previous three stages. When people talk about data-driven decision making, they are referring to the process of using data from I, T, and E and applying it to S. For example, you might identify three students to be writing mentors for another three students who didn't master a skill. You might schedule a meeting with teachers to strengthen their skill at asking higher-order thinking questions. You might plan an intervention for ELL students. Ideally, once you have a clear diagnosis of needs, the rest of your data analysis meeting will live in this stage.

Setting next steps is not just about adding something to your to-do list; it is about practicing and preparing. A strong coach will use this time to help a teacher plan out the next lesson. A data-driven team will use this time to talk through exactly how they'll reteach a skill, including who specifically needs the support, what exactly they will say to students, and how they will respond to misconceptions. A leader will return to the budget or school schedule to make adjustments in the moment that will facilitate follow-up actions regarding a concerning schoolwide trend. See Figure 1.1 for a BITES template you can use.

> **Apply:** *If you use data protocols, take a moment to pull one up. How does BITES show up in the protocol? Which component(s) of BITES do you emphasize the most in your data work?*

Little BITES Aren't Enough

BITES is a great start, but it's only the beginning for those who seek to infuse equity into data work in schools. Data work must go deeper and bake equity into its core operating system. Equity can and should be part of *all* stages of our data work, from preparing to gather data, to gathering and analyzing data, to doing something with the data. Unfortunately, we rarely see equity included in data protocols, and we rarely see equity centered in conversations about data. Most schools use BITS (leaving out the E), but adding the E isn't enough. We need to move from tossing equity into our data protocols to building an entire equitable data culture in our schools.

FIGURE 1.1 • BITES Template

Purpose: Analyze data from some or all students in the class.

Prework: Organize student data so it is easily accessible.

Bar: What is the expectation for students with this specific task? *Consider the standard, exemplar response, and/or definition of* mastery.	2–5 min
Individuals: What do individual students already know? What are they struggling with? *Look for patterns of successes, errors, and misconceptions within individual student responses.*	10–15 min
Trends: What do most students already know? What are most students struggling with? *Consider patterns across student responses.*	5–10 min
Equity: What inequities are showing up? *Consider race/ethnicity, gender, IEP status, ELL status, etc.*	5–15 min
Steps: What instructional changes/adjustments will move students? *Consider specific changes to how you'll teach individuals, groups, and/or the whole class. Practice!*	5–20 min

Figure 1.2 shows the Framework for Equitable Data Culture (EDC), which is an expanded set of equitable practices that can be spread across any data analysis work leaders engage in. It is not a replacement for BITES or the data protocol you might be using. Building an equitable data culture necessitates intentionally engaging in data work outside the protocols—before, during, and after your regularly scheduled data meetings. Ideally, this framework will help educators use data as the means to an equitable end rather than an end in itself.

FIGURE 1.2 • Framework for Equitable Data Culture

Step 1: Prepare Self and Team • Reflect on identities • Understand systemic inequity • Integrate bias-reduction strategies	
Step 2: Gather Data That Matters • Collaborate with the school community • Set an equitable purpose • Center experiences of minoritized groups	Apply Equitable Data Principles
Step 3: Engage in Asset-Based Analysis • Set intentions and agreements and address problematic mindsets • Pull out trends and elevate stories • Stay inquisitive	
Step 4: Take Action for Sustained Equity • Direct resources equitably • Make public commitments • Persevere through challenges	

This chapter provides an overview of EDC, and each stage of the process is described in more detail throughout the book. We encourage you to pause now and read the four steps of the framework and think about what each step currently looks like to you. With which do you feel confident? Which sound new? With which might you need practice to get stronger? As you read, try to maintain curiosity when you see familiar ideas or concepts. As you encounter new concepts, focus on potential applications by asking, "How can I put this into practice, given my role?"

An equitable data culture applies to all types of data. This includes the data teachers and leaders gather in classrooms, student work teachers analyze in PLCs, professional development feedback, interactions with families, and so much more. It is also broadly applicable. It is not used exclusively for reviewing student work or making sense of spreadsheets but instead is a process educators can constantly employ as they interpret the infinite, everyday, in-the-moment data they encounter. It can be used by school leaders to focus schoolwide strategy conversations around equity. A teacher could review the framework in the morning before students arrive or right after a troubling moment in class. A principal might review this framework before interviewing a teaching candidate or during a school-level data review. An instructional coach might use the framework while observing a classroom or to reflect on a recent coaching conversation. A dean might review it before calling a student's home. In other words, it serves as a constant reminder to put equity front and center.

EDC Step 1: Prepare Self and Team

The first step is both the most important and the easiest to skip over: prepare yourself and your team. Whenever you gather a team or work with a particular group in the school community, reflect on the identities of everyone involved. Start with yourself, then the team you are working with, and finally the people who are the focus of the analysis. Next, consider the systems at play. How do systemic inequalities intersect with this problem? In what ways are you at risk of enabling the inequitable system? How are you positioned to be an interrupter of the system? Finally, address biases head-on with bias reduction strategies.

Reflect on Identities

Reflect on your identities. Reflect on team members' identities. Reflect on students' and community identities. Examine how these identities inform beliefs and behaviors. It can be easy to think of data analysis as objective or separated from the self. However, data is not self-evident; data only speaks through individual interpretations. Leaders need an awareness of the lens through which they examine data. Our individual identities, as well as our data team's collective identities, inform our preferences, biases, and knowledge gaps. A group of monolingual English-speaking teachers might not understand why some of their Spanish-speaking kindergarteners are struggling with the /y/ sound, whereas a dual-language teacher might immediately know how to bridge the two languages in the classroom. Without an understanding of ourselves and our beliefs, we risk hurting others by bringing less awareness and empathy to our work.

You can learn more about your own identities by reflecting on your race, gender, age, first language, sexual orientation, and socioeconomic status. You might fill out a social identity wheel (Pabdoo, 2020)—a tool for identifying a range of visible and hidden identity markers—or write your racial autobiography, a reflective exploration into your racial experiences (Whites for Racial Equity, 2022). After everyone has individually spent time reflecting on their own lenses and identities, it is time to come together and reflect on the commonalities, differences, and power dynamics that exist within a team. The aim is to get a better understanding of where everyone is coming from as individuals and then identify which perspectives are well-represented and which might be missing or going unheard. Keep in mind that conversations about identity may be more painful for marginalized individuals or groups. For example, many teachers do not disclose queer identities because they fear discrimination. Staff should not be pressured to share anything overly personal or be expected to speak for an entire group to which they belong—or with which they identify.

Reflecting on identities is a starting point, not an end point. Challenge yourself to adapt—based on what you learn about yourself and your team—and to revisit the conversation often. For some teams, interrogating identities can feel uncomfortable and overly personal, and they are relieved once the conversation is over and seldom look back to it. For other teams, reflecting on identities is cathartic and can lead to overly tidy "aha" moments that come with a sense of accomplishment. In both cases, the true power of the conversation comes *after* the conversation. How are leaders balancing the power dynamics of the team? How are team members addressing their own problematic mindsets?

Understand Systemic Inequity

Understand systemic inequity, where it comes from, and your personal and team's collective positionality/complicity with it. Deepen your awareness of racism, sexism, classism, homophobia, transphobia, ableism, and other forms of oppression. In addition to zooming in on yourself and your team, you need to zoom out and understand the system within which you work.

The education system in the United States is an inequitable system. Every school contributes to that system in some way. By understanding the problems that exist in the larger system, you can figure out how your school contributes to those problems, along with the ways your school can be part of the solution. Some leaders are eager to point to the ways they strive toward a solution and find it frustrating to learn how their school echoes the same inequities we see nationwide. Some leaders try to distance themselves from responsibility, saying, "But that's a societal problem everywhere." Instead, they could (and, perhaps, should) ask, "How does my school perpetuate society's inequities?" If we see patterns of inequity at the national level, those patterns are rooted in individual schools and classrooms.

Schools are also matrixed with other unfair systems that can undermine the purpose of schools. Residential segregation creates racially and socioeconomically segregated schools. Unfair tax policies often mean that a larger share of public dollars go to schools that need them the least. Educators cannot be charged with fixing all the societal forces that curtail opportunities for kids based on where they were born. However, learning how other systems affect students' life chances can strengthen the supports students receive while at school.

Any form of inequity we can name becomes an inequity we can work to address and prevent. A principal who understands the school-to-prison pipeline might become more critical of school disciplinary practices and put extra effort into preventing disparities in discipline. A school sunshine committee that understands the importance of retaining teachers of color will ensure staff events and celebrations are culturally relevant. Each layer of awareness empowers leaders to adjust their practice appropriately.

There are plenty of ways to learn about systemic oppression. We can memorize and share statistics (see Virtual Appendix A, ascd.org/Equity InDataAppendix.pdf). We can take classes, read books, listen to podcasts, follow social media accounts, and watch documentaries about the history and contemporary persistence of inequity. We can listen carefully when people who have identities we don't share volunteer their lived experiences with oppression (without burdening them to be "oppression educators"). We can continue to interrogate why inequities exist and reframe the question to include both our own complicity and the policies inside and outside our sphere of influence.

Integrate Bias-Reduction Strategies

Integrate bias-reduction strategies, such as stereotype replacement and increased positive contact, into structures and systems. Bias seeps into nearly every facet of our lives and is especially present in our data work. We are biased when we use data to subconsciously confirm our beliefs, exclusively use less complicated data, or draw conclusions from data about a person's innate character. An assistant principal who has internalized the false stereotype that girls are smarter than boys might unconsciously approve more female applicants for a gifted-and-talented program. Conversely, a hiring team might mitigate their implicit biases against people of color by proactively adding a step to the interview process in which the team only describes positive qualifications of candidates of color for the first five minutes.

We have opportunities every day to recognize biased mindsets and change biased policies, all in service of making our schools more equitable. The more we integrate bias-reduction strategies into our data practices *prior* to engaging in data collection and analysis, the fewer opportunities we give bias to join us on the journey.

To curb the impact bias has on exacerbating inequity, we must first build an awareness of the various types of biases (see Virtual Appendix C, ascd.org/EquityInDataAppendix.pdf) and where and when they show up in ourselves and our work. Taking an implicit association test is a good starting point (Project Implicit, 2011). We must also replace negative stereotypes with positive images and create increased opportunities for positive contact and associations.

EDC Step 2: Gather Data That Matters

All schools have data they are obligated to collect by law or district mandate, but they typically have more leeway in how they *use* the data collected. In addition to compliance data, schools gather many streams of other data that are not required, which might include teacher-created exit tickets, staff satisfaction surveys, or informal notes about students. In this step, we invite you to think critically about the (nonmandatory) data you choose to gather and how you use both compliance and noncompliance data to make decisions. Before changing your data collection practices, consult your district's policies on data collection, particularly when it comes to students.

Data collection can easily fall into the trap of "data colonizing," in which data collection is extractive rather than beneficial to the participants. In other words, we often take more than we give in data work; we extract information from students through overtesting, we extract data from teachers with inefficient paperwork processes, and so on. The damage of data colonizing is typically twofold. First, it wastes participants' time during the data collection stage; second, it fails to meet participants' needs because the data collection tool does not consider their perspective. Extractive data collection is surprisingly common. For example, student assessments have the potential to be extractive when they use up a lot of students' time but don't end up providing much benefit to the students themselves.

The antidote to data colonization is community-centered data collection. Work with the data participants or respondents, such as teachers, families, and students, to agree on which data should be gathered and prioritized. Ask, "What data matters most? What data is most meaningful to *you*? What is our purpose for gathering these data?" Collectively identify the purpose for the data work and make an explicit connection to how the data should reveal disparities during data analysis. Purposeful and equitable data collection focuses on people over numbers. Instead of using more historically prioritized data, such as test scores, center the feelings, perspectives, and experiences of minoritized groups and individuals.

Collaborate with the School Community

Collaborate with members of the school community who are the data participants and respondents, such as teachers, families, and students, when determining which data to prioritize. We won't know if the data we're gathering matter unless we are working with the data participants to determine what we should gather. We must work *with* others instead of doing things *for* or *to* them. It's a simple concept but infrequently applied to data work, which has traditionally been colonial in nature. An instructional coach that coaches a teacher in areas the teacher does not want to develop will likely see little progress. By contrast, a high school literature teacher might review the syllabus with students and invite input from families through a survey when settling on books to read and topics to teach. Such conversations have the potential to transform the assessment data the teacher will examine during the school year—and the data will be more reflective of the community the teacher is serving.

To effectively collaborate with the school community, we must commit the time at the front end to meet with them. Form a data team that consists of representatives of the respondents, such as a teacher advisory board that helps design and analyze professional development surveys alongside the facilitator. Collaboration and coalition building don't have to be limited to this second step in the EDC; working with the school community informs our understanding of everyone's identities (Step 1), adds nuance and humanity to data analysis (Step 3), and holds everyone accountable to the committed actions we take (Step 4).

Set an Equitable Purpose

Set an equitable purpose for data collection that will reveal inequuities during data analysis. This means setting equitable goals and designing questions that specifically illuminate disparities. We too often disconnect the purpose for data collection from equity. We do this, for example, when we gather data that can't be disaggregated by subgroup or when we lump all students together in our academic goals. An instructional coach might tell the math department to focus on progress monitoring the "bubble kids" because of pressure from administration to move students into "proficient" on the state test, ultimately resulting in an educational disinvestment among the students who are struggling the most. On the other hand, a dean in charge of monitoring schoolwide attendance might focus attendance data collection and initiatives on the 15 percent of students with the lowest attendance, intentionally directing resources where they are needed. Who and what we focus our attention on can just as easily create or erase the opportunity to redress inequity.

In setting an equitable purpose, leaders should name specific prioritized subgroups about whom they will gather data. At the school level, equitable goals must address the big picture and be set up to mitigate significant issues in the school community. They should not target one-off or bite-sized obstacles that appear to further equity but in reality have no positive transformative impact. With an equitable purpose for data collection, leaders will be more likely to use tools like an equity audit or a White supremacy culture assessment, which are described in the next chapter.

Center Experiences of Minoritized Groups

Center the feelings, perspectives, and experiences of minoritized groups and individuals. This means focusing on the people most likely to be harmed by school policies or inaction. This does not mean burdening minoritized individuals in the building with additional tasks. A leadership team might talk to cisgender and straight students about their mindsets about LGBTQIA+ people as they plan to address problematic mindsets that might harm LGBTQIA+ youth in the building. Often, however, leaders should speak directly to the people whom they wish to support in order to meet their needs. For example, school leaders who sense dissatisfaction in the biliteracy program might hold a focus group for dual-language teachers.

Surveys, empathy interviews, and focus groups are just a few key data-gathering tools at our disposal that center experiences. In addition, tapping into the opinions and perspectives of families can unearth narratives to which school leaders would have been oblivious. In instructional observation, we should spend more time talking to students and teachers rather than using checklists. As we gather data, both formally and informally, we must always ask ourselves if we are putting people first.

EDC Step 3: Engage in Asset-Based Analysis

The third step is to examine and interpret data through an equity lens. EDC keeps our analysis asset-based and avoids blaming an individual or group for results we perceive to be worrisome, while also recognizing our own complicity and accountability for results. As we analyze data, we examine both trends and outliers so we can include all respondents in the conclusions we draw. We also look at data through an asset-based—or even better, a gifted—lens, wondering, "What knowledge and skills have students learned?" or "What school policies and programs yield satisfaction and engagement from families?" This step includes the moments right before we look at data, when we set intentions and agreements for the exploration, and how we address mindsets that detract from equitable interpretation.

Set Intentions and Agreements and Address Problematic Mindsets

Set intentions prior to analysis and set equity-focused agreements. Identify and address data traps and problematic mindsets as they come up. These up-front actions often prevent problematic mindsets and behaviors from getting in the way of meaningful data analysis. Intention setting creates a space for people to look inside and reflect on how they are feeling and what they are bringing to the meeting that may influence their participation in the dialogue (Aguilar, 2014). Intentions allow people to hold themselves accountable to a personal goal for a short time—often just for the duration of a meeting. Problematic mindsets may still surface during the process, and a combination of effective facilitation (for group analysis) and self-monitoring (for individual analysis) can help us navigate challenges. A teacher who has been made aware of their preferential treatment of students without IEPs might pause before students arrive and set an intention of allocating more 1:1 and small-group time to students with IEPs. A teacher leader might pause a data analysis meeting and start a critical discussion when they hear a colleague say, "I think looking at this data broken down by race is a waste of time. There are factors that are more important than race."

Team building and building a culture of learning and vulnerability will help unearth biased mindsets and empower teams to tackle them collaboratively. A simple agreement in PLCs such as "We talk about students as if they are with us in the room" can quickly shift the type of discourse during data analysis to asset-based and optimistic language.

Pull Out Trends and Elevate Stories

Pull out trends in the data to determine successes and concerns. Elevate the stories and experiences that challenge your expectations, including those that appear to be outliers in the data. This is the *I* and *T* of BITES. The examination of data involves pulling out trends and patterns, as well as paying attention to outliers or individual stories that might otherwise get sidelined or ignored. A 1st grade team reviewing a phonics diagnostic might notice that 96 percent of students know their letter sounds and that most kids are struggling with the *th* digraph. That team might plan to focus on teaching digraphs in the coming week, but they also note that one student (the child who represents the remaining 4 percent) is still learning consonant sounds. The team can use this information to plan individual instruction for that child. The trend informs the full-group actions, and the outliers inform the individual or small-group supports. We identify trends by looking for repeated occurrences in data and noticing patterns across data points. Data-tracking tools and data organization systems help bring these patterns to light.

Stories and individual experiences are key data we must use to supplement the patterns we see in the numbers. Typically, numbers can highlight a problem, but speaking to people about their experiences can help us arrive at solutions to those problems. We can have open discussions with students and families about the trends we see in the data to gain insight into the *why* behind the numbers. At a report card conference, we might learn that a parent wants strategies for how to help their child become more engaged with reading at home. Alternatively, we might learn that the parent has strategies that are working at home that haven't been tried in the classroom. As a result, the data led to the teacher adapting their approach and the family feeling better equipped with tools. It's win-win.

The best salespeople know that people are persuaded by stories, not by numbers. However, stories can be misused, and a powerful story can mask unimpressive or inequitable outcomes. As you incorporate the stories and experiences of families, teachers, and students into your data analysis practice, pay attention to the types of stories you fixate on and how those stories confirm or oppose your preconceived ideas about a problem. It can be easy to cherry-pick the stories and perspectives we want to hear, particularly when they come from a charismatic speaker. When you analyze qualitative data, it is helpful to ask, "Why am I focusing in on this trend? Are there other stories that conflict with this one? Does this idea confirm what I already thought to be true?"

Stay Inquisitive

Stay inquisitive by asking "Why?" and gathering follow-up data. Avoid playing the data blame game. Data analysis is an inherently inquisitive exploration. Too often, we default to drawing definitive conclusions from data, such as a child's capacity for learning or a teacher's effectiveness. We are always working with limited information, and data will never paint a full picture. A teacher might have a frustrating conversation with a parent and stop before writing the parent off as unsupportive or not invested in their child's learning, recognizing that the experience was just a single interaction. An assistant superintendent in charge of a network of schools might schedule a data meeting with the principals who had the most concerning data, not to apply pressure or reprimand them but to examine additional data that helps clarify how the school can improve.

Follow-up data can help us triangulate results or expand on initial findings. Sometimes staying inquisitive means spending more time with the data, but it also might involve readjusting our lens and paying attention to something we hadn't previously focused on. Our inquisitiveness means a healthy combination of taking ownership for results and acknowledging factors outside our sphere of influence. Exclusively blaming others or the system is rarely productive. Staying inquisitive elevates the humanity of participants and holds us to a higher bar than empathy.

EDC Step 4: Take Action for Sustained Equity

The fourth step is where we do something with the data we've analyzed. We redistribute resources, focus supports in a particular place or with a particular group, and hold ourselves accountable to follow through by making public commitments and making a plan that includes collective action. When we are met with obstacles along the way, we keep our eyes on the prize and persevere. In situations where additional data shifts our understanding of what's taking place, we might pivot or reset.

Direct Resources Equitably

Direct resources equitably based on subgroups that are specifically named in action items. A key part of acting for equity involves redistributing resources (e.g., time, money, personnel) based on subgroup. Unfortunately, leaders are often more comfortable setting goals around racial equity than they are reallocating resources by race. Claims of "reverse racism" or "preferential treatment" prevent leaders from taking action that actually results in equitable outcomes. A principal might hire another special education support teacher after noticing disparities in student outcomes in the special education department. A teacher leader might start a math club for 3rd grade girls who are underperforming and who replied on a survey that they thought math was for boys. We can redirect resources by specifically naming the group—often falling along lines of identity—that will receive different or additional support or attention.

Make Public Commitments

Our commitments to equitable change within the school community should be strong, specific, and public. These commitments are not about false gestures or virtue signaling; they are about creating collective accountability. Building off the examples in the previous section, the principal might hold a community meeting to share and discuss the rationale behind hiring a new special education teacher. Similarly, the teacher leader might share their plan with colleagues and ask them to check in every month to see how the math club is progressing. That teacher leader might also discuss the math club with their class in a morning meeting.

These types of commitments require us to have moral clarity around our work, especially since the public nature of the commitments inevitably stir up discomfort or pushback from the school community. Families of students without IEPs might not like to hear that resources are being directed away from their children. The 3rd grade boys might not like the idea that they are not invited to an exclusive club. The other 3rd grade teachers might express concern that the club feels like sexism. By shifting the battle against inequity into a public space, we are suddenly accountable for aligning our beliefs with our actions.

Persevere Through Challenges

Persevere through challenges. As needed, reset when you're off course or pivot to higher-impact actions as additional data provides more clarity. Even the biggest, boldest equity commitments can fizzle out quickly. That's why we must persevere through challenges and reset as a group when we go off course. The principal who plans to hire another special education teacher might need to remind the hiring committee of this priority when they recommend a highly qualified teacher who does not have a background in special education. The teacher leader running the math club might find that after a few weeks, only two of five girls are regularly attending, and they need to follow up with the other three girls to learn what's going on.

Gathering additional data—such as an informal check-in with the girls who aren't coming to math club—can help us make small adjustments that help us persevere through challenges. Returning to commitments that are publicly posted (e.g., at the top of the hiring committee's interview rubric) and reminding people of the *why* will help reorient everyone to the purpose. There will inevitably be some occasions where additional data illuminates new needs and requires you to pivot to higher-impact actions. Be careful that these aren't moments when a competing priority or initiative is simply getting in the way of your commitment.

> **Apply:** *Think about the data culture in your school. What steps of EDC show up in your culture? What steps would you like to strengthen?*

Conclusion: Stretching Our Thinking

The best data analysis should challenge our current practices and stretch our thinking. We know our schools are inequitable, but we have the tools within our grasp to do something about it. We just need to start asking better questions and looking for answers in better places. Like any framework, the Framework for Equitable Data Culture is best understood through concrete examples. Therefore, the rest of this book will zoom in on how EDC is applied to specific facets of the school community.

2

Schools: School Identity, Equity Audits, Goals, and Public Statements

*We never know how our small activities will affect others through the invisible fabric of our connectedness. In this exquisitely connected world, it's never a question of "critical mass."
It's always about critical connections.*

—Grace Lee Boggs

Disproportionality Discussion

In March of 2021, a school's leadership team met to review a report of publicly available student data showing disproportionality in their school. The data lived a few clicks away on the state website and in the Civil Rights Database (Civil Rights Data Collection, n.d.), but this was the first time the team had intentionally discussed the report. As principals, teacher leaders, counselors, and other school leaders read through the document prepared by their leadership coach, they grew increasingly concerned.

"Does this really mean the average student is outperforming our English language learners in every subject by as much as 20 percentage points?" one teacher asked. Another leader added, "I'm shocked that our Black students are suspended at nearly twice the rate." The school nurse spoke up: "This is a gut punch for me." A counselor noticed that boys were underperforming girls in language arts and that girls were under-performing boys in math, an example of societal stereotypes being lived out in the school. The principal concluded, "We need to figure out what to do with this information."

> Just three months later, the school launched an equity audit to kick off its planning of equity-focused changes to the school for the following school year. By looking at data through an equity lens, school leaders had the information they needed to steer the school in a new direction.

The U.S. Department of Education spends millions of dollars every year to collect detailed data on every public school. Some of that information includes statistics on teacher expertise, discipline outcomes, and academic outcomes. Where does your school or district fit?

1. Nationally, about 9 percent of teachers have fewer than three years teaching experience (Digest of Education Statistics, 2021). My school/district
   a. Is worse than the national trend.
   b. Closely matches the national trend.
   c. Is better than the national trend.

4. An extraordinary 24 percent of students who receive out-of-school suspensions are students with disabilities, whereas students with disabilities make up only 14 percent of all students (Civil Rights Data Collection, 2016; Hussar et al., 2020). My school/district
   a. Is worse than the national trend.
   b. Closely matches the national trend.
   c. Is better than the national trend.

4. The national White–Hispanic test score gap is nearly two grade levels wide (Reardon & Fahle, 2017). My school/district
   a. Is worse than the national trend.
   b. Closely matches the national trend.
   c. Is better than the national trend.

 Most school leaders struggle to answer these questions. You are not a walking fact sheet, and that's OK. The point of this exercise is to connect inequity in your school to systemic inequity at a national level. Even if you don't know the exact numbers, you might have a good guess as to whether your school is better, worse, or on par with national trends.

EDC1 National trends are a great starting point for thinking about systemic inequity in your school. Thousands of experts, thousands of hours, and

millions of dollars have been poured into tracking inequity in education at the national level. Therefore, if you want to look at inequity in your school, paying attention to what's going on nationally is a great place to start. The previous examples are three dimensions of inequity that are of immense concern nationwide and thus likely also a concern at your school.

If you work in a public school, your school is one of the building blocks in those national numbers. This means you contribute to the national trends, for better or worse. If you work in a nonpublic or non-traditional school, it is still worthwhile to see where your school fits within the national numbers, but you may also have network-level numbers that would be more helpful for your specific context. Schools with a specialized focus, such as alternative schools and juvenile justice centers, may find it more helpful to look only at comparable schools rather than use traditional schools for comparison.

DP9

There is a gap—which sometimes feels more like a canyon—between the national and local conversations about inequity in schools. The national numbers may feel distant, whereas the local story is unique and full of nuance, history, and context. Take an honest look at how your local story contributes to the national education landscape. This is not meant to shame or frustrate but to inform and inspire change. We need courageous school leaders who own their part of the national story and shed light on what they need to build a more just and equitable education system.

ISPD

If there is an equity issue at your school (and, unfortunately, there probably is), chances are that you inherited the problem rather than created it. Still, it is your responsibility to shoulder the burden of addressing the issue. If you find that you cannot fix it, then your responsibility is to wield a megaphone and fight for what you need to fix. Many school leaders already walk this path and embrace their role as both leader and advocate. It is not an easy path, but it is a necessary one.

Our resp to shoulder the burden ↓ wield a megaphone

Indeed, the pursuit of equity in school begins with school leaders who need to make their commitment to equity visible to students, staff, and families. This helps everyone feel empowered to join in the equity work and speak up when they think the work veers off track.

In this chapter, we offer guidance for leaders as they dive into equity work at their school(s). We won't cover every facet of the work, which can take on many different forms, but we offer four "buckets" of equity

*ISPD

leadership that are a solid start for the equity-minded leader: school identity, equity audits, goal setting, and public statements.

School Identity

IS PD

Every school has a unique identity that can change over time. Understanding that identity is the first step to creating an equitable environment for students and staff. In this section, we ask you to think about school identity from two vantage points: (1) the perspectives and values of the communities within your school, and (2) how your school is

EDC1 situated in comparison to peer schools.

Data from Your School Community

The foundation of every school is its people. Before beginning the complex work of surfacing equity issues, you need a baseline understanding of the communities within your school: families, students, support staff, teachers, administrators, and other members of the school community. When deepening your understanding of the people in a school, it's important to prioritize the voices of people with marginalized identities, such as teachers of color, students with disabilities, and

EDC2 family members with a history of low participation in school events.

You may already be able to identify which voices might otherwise get lost if you do not specifically seek them out. Alternatively, you might ask around to learn which voices are traditionally centered and

DP10 which are marginalized within your school context. Understanding the perspectives of those who might otherwise be left out of the dominant narrative is an important step toward building an equitable school community in which all members feel supported, regardless of identity or background.

Listening to the unique perspectives of the people within your school sounds deceptively simple, but it is lifelong work. It doesn't matter how long you have been a leader in a school or district; you are never done listening to community voices. There are two conversational structures that help leaders actively listen to the school community:

- **Listening Sessions:** A listening session (also known as a focus group) is an informal opportunity for a small group of people to share thoughts and feelings about their experiences and beliefs about the school. A listening session is typically semistructured, which means the leader structures the conversation with a list of questions but allows the conversation to flow naturally, depending on participants' contributions. If you are unsure where to start in a listening session, try adapting the strong but flexible SWOT framework (Strengths-Weaknesses-Opportunities-Threats) for the session:

- What do you think are the **strengths** and **weaknesses** of this school?
- Are there any **opportunities** you think the school should take?
- What do you see as external **threats** to the school?

This framework typically gives participants the flexibility to talk about what they love about a school, what they want to change, what they wish for the school, and what they worry about. The open-ended nature of the questions allows participants to take the lead and bring up what is most important to them.

- **Empathy Interviews:** An empathy interview is a listening session between two people, and it can be structured much like a listening session. It is a chance to better understand the perspective of one individual. An empathy interview is more appropriate than a group listening session when you are discussing sensitive topics or when you want to hear from someone who might be uncomfortable speaking publicly or honestly in a group setting.

Data About Your School Context

In addition to hearing directly from community members, looking at school data helps you understand the identity of a school. What are the demographics of your students, staff, and families? Does your school reinforce or counteract the systemic inequities that plague most public schools?

Figure 2.1 includes sample metrics to see how your school or district compares to national trends. Spend some time considering the demographics of your school, then consider how your school measures up to common symptoms of systemic inequity. It's important to point out that these quantitative metrics are not intended to replace or be more important than the qualitative experiences of members of the school community captured in listening sessions and empathy interviews.

FIGURE 2.1 • Compare Your School/District with National Trends

Metric	National Average[1]	Your School/District
% Living in poverty	18%	
% With disabilities	12%	
% English language learners	10%	
% Native American/Alaska Native	1%	
% Asian	5%	
% Black	15%	
% Hispanic or Latinx	27%	
% White	48%	
Black–White test score gap[2]	• 4th grade reading: ~2 grade levels • 4th grade math: ~2½ grade levels • 8th grade reading: ~2½ grade levels • 8th grade math: ~2½ grade levels	
Hispanic–White test score gap[2]	• 4th grade reading: ~2 grade levels • 4th grade math: ~2 grade levels • 8th grade reading: ~2 grade levels • 8th grade math: ~2 grade levels	
% Suspension rate for students with disabilities[3]	24%	
% Suspension rate for Black students[3]	• 18% for Black boys • 10% for Black girls	
% Teachers of color[1]	21% of public school teachers	
% Gifted-and-talented students who are White[3]	57%	

[1]Hussar et al., 2020; [2]Reardon & Fahle, 2017; [3]U.S. Civil Rights Data Collection, 2016.

We don't expect you to change any of these metrics overnight; that would make you a superhero. These metrics are simply meant to get you started.

> **Apply:** *Where is there inequity in your school, and how does your school compare to the national picture? In what ways do you have power or influence—at least on some level—to address those inequities?*

use this question

From School Identity to Action

Reflecting on school identity can sometimes feel like too much reflection and too little action. This can be frustrating for leaders who are tired of talking about equity and are ready to *act*. Whenever a leader starts to feel that the balance of reflection-to-action weighs too heavily on the reflection end of the spectrum, there are two courses of action. First, never consider your reflection work done. People grow and change over time. The unique identities and power dynamics in your school will always need careful tending. Plan for how you will continue to weave identity work into the day-to-day structures of your team. Second, use **DP4** the reflection work you've done as a foundation for future actions you will take. As you move into the more action-oriented portions of this chapter, consider identity work to be an integral part of your actions.

② Equity Audits

CSPD

An equity audit is an investigation into equity at your school—and should be seen as a learning opportunity for leaders. Despite the pejorative connotation of the word *audit*, Terrance Green (2016) points out that the root of the word *audit* is the Latin word *audire*, which means "to listen/hear" (other words in the same family are *auditory*, *audio*, and *audience*). In the process of an equity audit, leaders listen to the perspectives of staff, students, and families and identify the ways their school reinforces inequitable patterns present in society at large. After an equity audit, you might find that you think about the power dynamics and relationships in your school in different ways.

Defined questions drive audits.

EDC2 Equity audits are typically grounded in broadly defined questions, such as "How can we make this school a more equitable place for students?" or "How can we be an antiracist school?" These foundational questions are broadly defined so the equity audit can cast a wide net and identify inequity where leaders might not expect it. After centering your equity audit around a question, the information gathering begins,

EDC2 which can consist of document reviews, interviews, focus groups, surveys, and more traditional forms of data analysis (e.g., student assess-

DP5 ments). Figure 2.2 provides options to begin the auditing process.

FIGURE 2.2 • Three Sample Processes for Equity Audits

Using equity audits to create equitable and excellent schools (Skrla et al., 2009)	*The equity audit as the core of leading* (Capper et al., 2020)	*Community-based equity audits* (Green, 2016)
1. Create a committee of relevant stakeholders. 2. Present the data to stakeholders. 3. Discuss the meaning within the data. 4. Find and plan potential solutions. 5. Implement solutions. 6. Evaluate the results. 7. Celebrate success or return to Step 3.	1. Attain proportional representation. 2. Establish a team. 3. Design the audit. 4. Gather and analyze data. 5. Set goals. 6. Plan for implementation.	1. Disrupt deficit views of community. 2. Conduct a community inquiry. 3. Assemble a community leadership team. 4. Gather asset-based community data for action.

DP10 An external organization with equity audit expertise and an "outsider" perspective is an excellent choice for any school that can afford it. They take care of the administration of the equity audit so leaders can fully participate and focus on the content rather than the logistics. An external provider also has expertise and will be able to notice patterns that someone who is new to equity audits might miss.

However, external equity audits can be expensive, and the reality is that schools cannot always fit them into their budgets. For these schools, we encourage an internal equity audit led by someone in your school community. What a school insider might lack in relevant experience, they make up for with an intimate knowledge of the school environment. External objectivity in equity audits can be an overrated, Westernized ideal. An external consultant must spend a lot of time getting up to speed on school dynamics, so having a school leader or partner participate directly in data collection can be a bridge-building experience between the equity audit leader and community members. For example, when principals run focus groups, they get to hear directly from their staff—and the staff get additional facetime with the principal.

A note of caution is warranted here. Too much insider knowledge of a school can also lead to confirmation bias. Someone who is internal to the school will likely have built-up assumptions based on personal experiences. They may accidentally use an equity audit to confirm preconceived ideas about what needs to change in the school. This is a misuse of an equity audit. There is no foolproof way to avoid confirmation bias, so it's important to pay extra attention to new ideas and perspectives that contradict your own. You might successfully avoid confirmation bias if you feel a little outside your comfort zone or if you find that the equity audit process is taking your school in a different direction from the one you might have taken without it.

In the following sections, we describe two sample equity audits that were run by school-based staff. Both center race and racism in schools, but the same processes could apply to any other equity lens. We highlight these two very different examples to demonstrate how a leadership team might make use of their current team and regularly scheduled PD time to run an equity audit. As much as we encourage schools to invest in expert equity consultants, we hope to demonstrate that you don't have to wait until there's room in the budget to get started.

Equity Audit 1: Identifying Priorities

In August of 2020, building off the momentum of international protests against racial injustice, five schools and their leadership teams conducted high-level equity audits with the support of coauthors Michael and Andrew. The equity audits took place during a single three-hour workshop, but they were the culmination of an entire year of coaching leaders around equity. What follows are the steps the schools took to identify high-level school equity priorities.

Frame the conversation. In all meetings and professional development sessions, but especially when talking about racial equity, the

EDC3 facilitator must frame the conversation effectively. Andrew began by naming two things that wouldn't be up for discussion:

- Racism is real. Racism, White supremacy, anti-Blackness, and other forms of oppression exist in U.S. society and our schools.
- Antiracism is our responsibility. Our work as educators and humans is directly connected to race, racism, equity, and antiracism.

This common ground helped push the conversation beyond a deflective discussion that might question what should be common knowledge. If anyone didn't agree with those two statements, Andrew encouraged them to "take a listener stance today and reach out after the session so we can talk more." This pushed those who disagreed both to engage in the session and to seek support.

Michael then reviewed some community agreements for conversations about race, adapted from *Courageous Conversations About Race* (Singleton, 2015) and other texts:

- **Engage:** Conversations about race are triggering and challenging for most people. Please stay present and engaged throughout.
- **Take care of yourself:** Stay hydrated. Breathe and exhale. If it's virtual, it's OK to turn off your camera. If it's in-person, it's OK to step out of the room or ask for a one-on-one check-in with a facilitator.
- **Open up:** Our learning is so much greater when we hear vulnerable reflections, experiences, feelings, and stories from one another. This is a safe space to say something negative about yourself. This is not a place to "cover your racist tracks."
- **Lean into discomfort:** We tend to see discomfort as a negative, but discomfort is usually a signal that we are on the cusp of learning something new.

Afterward, he asked if there were any other agreements participants wanted to add before transitioning the group to the equity audit. Here is what he shared:

Why should we conduct an equity audit of our schools? I like to think of an equity audit as putting on equity glasses. It's about making the invisible visible, talking about a reality in our schools that is often either overlooked or ignored. Some of you have had on your equity glasses most of your life, others might have equity glasses that don't fit well or aren't the right prescription or distort your vision, and some of you may have just put them on and are getting used to the feel.

Regardless of where you are in your ability to recognize inequities in the school, an equity audit of our work helps us (1) look at some of the areas of our own practice we might not examine enough—because of space, time, capacity, interest, or awareness; (2) identify strengths and gaps where we can make our schools more equitable; and (3) make concrete, accountable plans and commitments to enacting changes in our school.

Conduct an independent audit. Participants then independently completed the following eight-question survey about their school on a 1–5 scale (1 = Not at all, 3 = Somewhat accurate, 5 = Perfect description). The survey included space for open-ended comments about each item in addition to the numerical rating.

- Overall, the school has prioritized equity and antiracism in its vision, values, strategic plan, and budget.
- The school recruits, hires, and retains a diverse group of teachers whose identities are reflective of students.
- School teams use an equity lens when gathering and analyzing data.
- School safety and disciplinary practices emphasize student freedom and restorative practices.
- Families have frequent access to information about their child's progress.
- Families have opportunities to weigh in on school decisions.
- Signage and nomenclature throughout the school are bias-free, are welcoming, and reflect diverse identities.
- Educators use equity-focused, culturally responsive teaching practices.

Engage in group discussion. School teams then transitioned to discussion. They reviewed the results of the survey, and Andrew encouraged them to focus on two things.

Place yourself in the position of power. Avoid saying, "Teachers should…" or "Once admin does…" or "The district needs to…" Instead, use *I* and *we*. That means taking responsibility for change, not pushing it onto someone else. Second, embrace "good trouble," in the words of the late Congressman John Lewis. We need to be honest and vulnerable about the change that is necessary to make our schools more equitable. Lewis reminded us that we need to be noisemakers and disrupters, challenging the status quo and creating trouble in order to make change.

DP10 Teams then discussed priorities, based on their ratings. Michael prompted them to focus on both areas of agreement and areas where opinions diverged. (See Chapter 5 for details on the interrater reliability process.)

Conduct research and explore further learning. Finally, teams explored an accompanying document with a number of suggested actions and linked resources on organizational culture, staff hiring, data, discipline, family engagement, signage, and professional learning (see Virtual Appendix E, ascd.org/EquityInDataAppendix.pdf). The ses-**EDC4** sion ended with commitments to next steps. Each school selected areas of improvement and used a combination of the provided resources and their own ideas to determine next steps that made sense for their context. Some leaders focused on teacher recruitment, whereas others decided to strengthen their restorative disciplinary practices. One school even decided to apportion a part of its budget to a more comprehensive external equity audit the following year.

Equity Audit 2: Assessing White Supremacy Culture

Our second equity audit example comes from a public elementary school that didn't have the budget to pay an external consultant to conduct an equity audit. The school wanted to take a deep dive into how it was upholding the interpersonal and systemic racism that permeates the rest of society. The school partnered with coauthors Andrew and Kendall to assemble an equity audit team of three members of the school community who worked within the school: the education leadership coach (Andrew), the school literacy specialist, and a teacher **EDC2** leader from the school. They were joined by two external experts who volunteered their time: a researcher (Kendall) and an additional education leadership coach who had expertise in equity work.

This team developed an equity audit tool to assess staff culture, specifically how it was upholding White supremacy or forwarding antiracism. The tool was inspired by an article many teachers in the building had already encountered, which is a clear breakdown of characteristics you might find in your workplace that are not overtly racist in nature but are still symptoms of a culture informed by White supremacy (revised as Okun, 2021).

An example that highlights White supremacy culture in the workplace is "quantity over quality" and the Western drive to push toward measurable goals at the expense of quality. The equity audit tool also drew on a series of questions and indicators adapted from a range of publications, including *Transforming Organizational Culture Assessment Tool* (Potapchuk, 2021) and *White Women Doing White Supremacy in Nonprofit Culture* (Talley, 2019).

The team broke down the components of White supremacy culture that play out in schools and dreamed up their positive counterparts: the components of antiracist culture. With that information in hand, they developed a tool that juxtaposes the two cultures (Figure 2.3).

This framework went through several rounds of feedback with school leaders and teachers before it reached the version you see here. Each bullet point became a survey question that was asked of all staff using a 5-point Likert scale (from *strongly agree* to *strongly disagree*) that was administered through Google Forms (see Virtual Appendix F, ascd.org/EquityInDataAppendix.pdf). For the analysis, the raw data was **DP6** converted into graphs via Google Sheets—no fancy software necessary. Each question was also broken out by subgroup: by self-reported race **DP8** and by school role.

The team then examined each chart and wrote a brief analysis to **EDC3** summarize their interpretation. This ensured the analysis reflected local knowledge of the school and was fully "owned" by a part of the **EDC2** school community. Finally, each member of the analysis team took time to digest the findings and develop recommendations for the school: **DP10**

- Create an inclusive schoolwide procedure for handling microaggressions and discrimination.
- Create a public description of roles and responsibilities accessible to all staff and that clearly delineates how power is distributed.

ISPD

FIGURE 2.3 • White Supremacy School Culture Versus
Antiracist School Culture

White Supremacy School Culture	Antiracist School Culture
Paternalism • People in power are all or mostly White. • People in power make decisions without including others. • Relationships feel transactional. *Examples* • The leadership team is primarily composed of administrators. • Staff call students' homes without telling the student why. • The school creates an initiative for family engagement without including families in the planning process. • The principal communicates with staff using memos and includes "this is a directive" in that communication.	**Shared leadership** • The demographics of people in power reflect the served community. • Decision-making centers the experiences and input of those with less power. • Relationships with colleagues feel supportive. *Examples* • Staff explain logical consequences to students instead of doling out arbitrary punishments. • New policies include a request for feedback from staff. • Teachers lead PLCs and professional development sessions for their colleagues. • The principal holds regular office hours and encourages staff to bring questions and concerns. • Student leadership is present in classrooms and throughout the school.
Narrowness • It feels like there is one right way of operating. • Staff work in silos and value independence and individualism. • Staff usually work independently. *Examples* • The principal pressures instructional coaches to only use the district-created data analysis protocol in PLCs. • The school implements a new curriculum that one person has recommended without piloting it first. • After a frustrating day, the principal works late into the night developing a new school safety plan and emails it to staff as a directive.	**Multiple Paths to Success** • There are multiple right ways of operating. • Mistakes are seen as learning opportunities. • Staff have regular structures for collaboration. *Examples* • The schedule is structured so teachers have regular PLCs and other spaces to collaborate. • Leadership team meetings involve lively discussion, open brainstorming, and research sharing. • Teachers' and administrators' doors are either open or unlocked. Most meetings take place in visible spaces.

White Supremacy School Culture	Antiracist School Culture
Conflict Aversion • Communication from leadership is limited and lacks transparency. • People in power get defensive easily. • People in power try to change the subject when race, bias, or accountability are brought up. *Examples* • Teachers are regularly confused about what is going on and are afraid to speak up. • Supposedly collaborative spaces (such as PLCs) are dominated by administration sharing directives with teachers but saying very little. • When the principal hears about an issue in the school, they blame the issue on teachers or use individuals as scapegoats. • Teachers and coaches/evaluators have distrustful relationships, and the coaching/evaluation process results in defensiveness and disingenuous commitments.	**Open Communication** • Leadership communicates transparently with staff. • People in power demonstrate vulnerability. • People in power interrogate their own biases and openly discuss race and personal complicity. *Examples* • Coaches regularly engage teachers in feedback sessions, including upward feedback from the teacher to the coach. • The principal validates the emotions of an upset teacher and commits to providing additional support to that teacher. • The PLC facilitator pauses the meeting to make room for the group to troubleshoot a serious issue a teacher just brought up. • The post-evaluation debrief discussion between the assistant principal and teacher is an enjoyable and positive experience for both.
Expansion • There is a culture of urgency. • Equity-focused efforts are mostly performative. • There is a message to work beyond a reasonable work schedule. *Examples* • A new initiative to keep hallways safe lasts two weeks due to disorganized planning and limited buy-in. • An instructional coach facilitates a one-off professional development session on math standards based solely on feedback from a district walkthrough. • The school's "equity push" consists of one full-staff conversation about a current event followed by repeated reminders to "engage in equity work" without committing money, time, and planning energy into making actual changes.	**Patience** • The focus is on quality over quantity. • Equity-focused efforts disrupt inequity in the school. • Leaders prioritize people and their well-being. *Examples* • When the principal identifies a non-emergency concern in school data, they assemble colleagues to discuss possible solutions before jumping into action. • With input from key players, the school community develops and implements a 3-year strategic plan built around three equity-focused goals. • A school leader pushes back against the superintendent when they describe a new policy that will likely make it harder for the school to hire and retain teachers of color.

- Assemble and pay a cross-racial staff task force to make actionable recommendations to the leadership team for improving the experiences of staff of color.

The first two recommendations were procedural. The third was a continuation of the conversation—an inclusive call for future research. Remember, an equity audit is merely a starting place; it's an opportunity to gather around a specific problem and build momentum for change.

The results of this survey were mixed and even reflected negatively on school leadership. Be forewarned—this is what you should expect when conducting an equity audit: a little good news and a large helping of bad news. Education has equity issues, and you should expect those to surface in your data when you go looking for them.

In this particular equity audit, we decided it was best to share the data (and therefore some of the power of the data) with the school leaders and staff at the same time. Staff members were the ones who took the time to thoughtfully answer the survey questions, so they should have access to the results. In other research projects, it's typical to share the results with the leaders first so they can have a say in how the results will be distributed and so they will be ready to share out a plan for what they will do in response to the data. However, we felt that approach was top-down rather than collaborative. It should be mentioned that we were fortunate to have a school leader who was open to sharing the equity audit data with all staff before any detailed plans were made.

We gave careful thought to how we would frame the public conversation about the equity audit, and we arrived at the following language:

> This report captures real, lived experiences of staff at [School Name]. The 60 staff members who completed the survey did so with honesty and vulnerability, and their feedback deserves to be witnessed by and shared with school staff. This report is also inherently limited not only because of the small number of questions asked but also because we did not conduct empathy interviews or do further research into the dynamics playing out in the school community. We also do not include student and family or external perspectives, and our report does not include every qualitative response

or analysis of every question. The purpose of this report is to capture staff culture and dynamics and elevate the experiences of role groups and racial groups in order to make the school a safer, more equitable, antiracist, and inclusive space.

As these examples demonstrate, equity audits do not need to be elaborate affairs or require fancy consultants. Rather, they simply require concentrated, community engagement around the threats to equity in your school. They also require a commitment from school leaders that show they care about equity and will see their commitment to equity through by gathering data that matters.

> **Apply:** *What would it look like to use one of these equity audits in your school?*

what opportunities do we have to use equity audits?

ISPD

③ Goals

After completing an equity audit, it is time to set schoolwide goals based on what you learned. One common problem with school goals is that they rarely connect to the school vision, which is often aspirational. Indeed, vision statements sometimes sound like the following word scramble: "Provide a safe, inclusive, positive, stimulating environment that fosters, encourages, empowers and cares for children to achieve their fullest potential, accomplish their wildest dreams, and be lifelong learners, global thinkers, and successful citizens."

Many schools and districts start with lofty, belief-oriented ideas, and then we pair those statements with goals that only barely align. Goals sound like "Increase daily attendance by 5 percent" or "Improve math scores on the state test by 10 percent." They are narrow and measurable, but will improved performance on the standardized exam actually translate into helping children achieve their fullest potential? Probably not. Will it result in greater educational equity in the school? Unlikely.

What's missing is the throughline from vision to goals to strategy to metrics. With that in mind, let's look at two examples of what small-scale, equity-focused revisions to school goals could look like:

Example 1

Original goal: 80% of 3rd–5th graders will score proficient or advanced on the spring benchmark exam, up from 68% on the winter benchmark.

Revised goal with equity language: 80% of 3rd–5th graders will score proficient or advanced on the spring benchmark exam, up from 68% on the winter benchmark. No group of students based on race, gender, or IEP status will outperform their classmates.

Example 2

Original goal: We will improve schoolwide attendance by 5 percent in the 3rd quarter (baseline average of 88 percent).

Revised goal with equity language: We will improve attendance by 15 percent in the 3rd quarter for the 30 lowest-attending students (baseline average of 76 percent).

Notice how powerful the revised goals are. In Example 1, the added language creates an underlying commitment to equitable instructional practices. Teachers are encouraged to think explicitly about student diversity and are discouraged from simply focusing on the "bubble kids" **DP1** (i.e., the students who are just shy of proficiency). Similarly, in Example 2, the students with the worst attendance go from being at risk of being completely ignored to being the focal point for interventions and sup-**EDC4** ports. In addition, it's much easier to identify and implement supports for a group of 30 students than it is for the entire school. Example 1's revision models how equity language can make a goal more ambitious, and Example 2's revision models how equity language can make a goal more manageable.

The revised goals required a clear understanding of where inequity was currently playing out in the school. Without an investigation into data prior to setting the goal, it would be difficult to add equity language to the original goals. Yes, it's more work, but once goals are set around equity, there is a clear pathway for dismantling inequitable practices.

If you want to push goal setting beyond the traditional approaches, consider the following sample school priorities (rather than goals):

- Use an equity lens when planning curriculum, instruction, and school policies.

- Dramatically improve staff, student, and family engagement.
- Ensure that all students have daily access to standards-aligned, grade-level content and tasks.
- Implement a restorative practices approach to discipline.
- Improve the recruitment, morale, and retention of staff of color.

If you're familiar with SMART goals (an acronym for specific, measurable, attainable, results-oriented, and timebound), this list of priorities might set off alarm bells because they fail the SMART goal test. Sure, some of these priorities could be more specific or measurable, but we find that an obsession over metrics sometimes makes progress feel impossible (it's not likely that all families will constantly be engaged) or creates an arbitrary stopping point (such as thinking the work is done once 20 percent of your staff are people of color). We encourage you to release yourself and your school from the timebound, equity-neutral box of SMART goals and see how it feels. (Some organizations are now touting SMARTIE goals, with an *I* for *inclusive* and an *E* for *equity*, a change we applaud.)

Ultimately, goals and priorities are meant to be motivators, and big ideas are much better motivators than number thresholds. Consider how a school community might behave differently with open-ended equity priorities. They might have more room to innovate around how to achieve those priorities. They might act with more passion because they are inspired by the vision behind the priorities. They might seek out qualitative sources of information in addition to quantitative sources. In other words, they might have an honest reconciliation with data, deprioritizing the numbers and reprioritizing the people.

Shifting away from using SMART goals doesn't mean you stop looking at data. We won't eradicate inequities if we can't see them, and it's important to pressure-test new interventions and initiatives. Having a more expansive and qualitative goal should open you up to a larger variety of data. In addition to calculating the suspension rate as a stand-alone metric, you might bring in new—but equally meaningful—types of data to measure school culture, such as students' perceptions of safety and bullying. You might monitor the dean's responses to incidents or collect data on the degree and quality of implementation of restorative practices. Instead of centering a single metric, such as the suspension

DP5 rate (which can be fairly easily manipulated to show growth while little actually changes), monitor a variety of metrics.

DP10

Ultimately, keep your school priorities centered on values and big ideas rather than on specific numbers and metrics. Collect data to understand how new initiatives are working, but focus conversations and energy on the vision and values of the school.

> **Apply:** *Look at one of your current or upcoming school goals and rewrite it so it's more equitable.*

How can we help coaches guide teachers to create goals that promote equity?

④

ISPO

Public Statements

EDC4

School leaders should communicate where they stand on equity by making frequent and heartfelt public statements, which have a dual purpose. They inform the community of their thinking, and they solicit public input on their respective stances. Public statements are an opportunity for a conversation to begin and a chance for genuine feedback and growth.

Try this mini–equity audit around antiracist messaging. Search your email inbox and sent messages folder for the following words: *equity, inequity, racism, antiracism, justice.* Narrow your search further by filtering by sender, focusing on yourself and your supervisors. How many emails fit this search? Within those emails, how often are these concepts mentioned in a meaningful way? When one school leader engaged in this activity, he found that he hadn't mentioned any of these terms in three months, and the last mention was a reminder about "equity of voice" in professional development. Email isn't the only format for antiracist messaging, but it's definitely one key platform.

Some creators of data tools are also rethinking their public messaging. One educational software company, DeansList, is rewriting their data "core beliefs" to acknowledge the harm that data can have when used irresponsibly. In an interview, DeansList shared their draft language with us: "At its best, data is used to start conversations, motivate self-reflection, surface biases, identify successes, areas for growth, and progress, and ground decisions, action plans, and priorities. At its worst, data is used to evaluate, judge, reduce, prioritize compliance, and reinforce pre-existing ideas and stereotypes." Stewards of student data, such as school leaders, may want to adopt these core beliefs—which remind everyone working with student data that they have both immense power and responsibility—to publicly connect student data with equitable aims. Educators can use data equitably to fight bias and help students flourish, or they can use data inequitably to confirm preconceived harmful beliefs and reinforce stereotypes.

In 2017, Ames Community School District in Iowa disseminated a strong public statement taking ownership of the racial test score gaps in their schools. The public statement included a plan to train staff in cultural consciousness and districtwide academic goals specifically boosting the proficiency of Black students in the district. This first step kicked off three years of cultural consciousness training for staff, the hiring of a director of equity in 2019, two equity audits that same year, and the implementation of a districtwide Black Lives Matter at School Week of Action in 2021 (Ames Community School District, 2021). Taking the initial step of publicly naming inequity spurred years of tangible equity work.

Public statements can be words, but they should also be deeds, such as funding equity work. After making space for conversations about race in leadership team meetings, one elementary school principal in Philadelphia decided it was time to put her money where her mouth was. She apportioned the equivalent of 20 percent of a full-time role to hire an external equity consultant team to work with staff and analyze school data. This sent the message to school staff that equity was a formal priority for the school.

If you wait to talk about an equity issue until there is a critical incident at your school or in the news, then you've waited too long. Your antidiscrimination policies and values should be clear and on display well before incidents arise. This will also make it easier to respond to critical incidents of discrimination or harm in your community because you have already publicly declared where you stand. As we have mentioned, severe inequity is a societal reality; it will rear its ugly head in your school sooner or later in the form of a serious incident that you must address publicly. Being proactive about the school's values will only help the community healing begin more quickly in the aftermath of serious incidents.

Regrettably, many schools have clear, high-stakes opportunities to make public statements in support of equity and *still* choose not to make them. In the aftermath of racist behavior by White students, one Pennsylvania high school maintained a hard line of public silence on the issue to both the staff and community. White students had thrown a "ghetto-themed" party during which they mocked Black and Latinx culture and used racial slurs. Worse, Black and Latinx students were the ones who alerted administrators to the issue. School leaders declined to issue a public statement about the incident, and there exists no public record of whether the offending students faced any consequences. School leadership made the self-protective choice to stay neutral on a schoolwide racist incident.

In this case, of course, "neutrality" amounted to the tacit support of the racist status quo. If the school had issued a public statement, they could have publicly supported their Black and Latinx students. They also could have added momentum to the nationwide outcry that "racist" parties are unacceptable—and perhaps could have helped prevent future harm. After all, only the rare racist event is truly unique to one school; ghetto-themed parties have cropped up in high schools and colleges across the United States. Therefore, any serious instance of discrimination in your school is not unique to your building and is likely happening at many other schools throughout the country. A public statement to your community is the least you can do in the face of hate.

Here is a partial list of avenues you can pursue to share your school's commitment to equity and antiracism:

- Language on your school website
- Messages (including flags, symbols, and pictures) around the school building
- Emails and letters sent to families and staff
- School materials, including staff and student handbooks
- Communications with the press
- School budget

Conclusion: Hard Work and Heart Work

Many school leaders struggle to demonstrate the vulnerability and introspection required to open the door to a vision for racial justice work. That's because it's hard work. Indeed, it's both *hard* work and *heart* work. Leaders can get lost in the day-to-day and default to district-mandated goals that are built around the wrong metrics (such as suspensions and standardized test scores). It's easy to focus on what we've always done. It's easy to highlight what's going well, especially when you're trying to impress supervisors with your progress. But if we believe our system and our schools need to radically improve, then we need to step out of our comfort zones and publicly name our commitment to radical action.

3

Classrooms: The Gifted Lens and Student Data Conversations

If they cannot love and resist at the same time,
they will probably not survive.

—Audre Lorde, *Sister Outsider*

Posting Student Data

When I was teaching 5th grade, our data had to be posted with student ID numbers so everyone could see it. This is when I started hating data. We were a data-driven school in a turnaround network, and everything was based off data, which meant that we were expected to broadcast low scores to shame students into doing better. Instead, I tried to reframe the numbers. I used data to help and motivate my students, talking about data in positive ways and emphasizing that numbers can always change based on students' dedication to improving. I told students that they were better than a number. Now I don't post data like that but still have real conversations with students and use data to group them strategically.

—Zephrah Pam, teacher leader

There are many approaches to using data in schools. Some are transplanted from the corporate world to maximize results, some are for proving a track record of "turnaround success," some are cuffed to test scores for funding or renewal, and some are earnestly committed to being responsive. When seen as a means to an end, gathering and using data can easily become distorted and feel automated. Such approaches can be harmful in schools as they leave little room to acknowledge the human experience of data. In that landscape, experiences like Zephrah's are not uncommon.

Building an equitable data culture in the classroom begins with focusing on the humans in the classroom. How do teachers perceive students? What do school leaders do to frame or reframe teachers' beliefs about their students' innate abilities? How we see our students is how we treat our students, and how we treat our students informs **EDC1** how they see themselves. For educators who believe students are inherently flawed and need a teacher to show them what to do and how to do it, their classrooms will focus on themselves—a teacher as the primary actor—and view students as learning recipients. If educators focus on compliance, then classrooms become oriented around teacher control. This leaves little space for students' identities and humanity. By contrast, if educators feel supported in upholding students' natural talents, they will be better equipped to see students' essential, powerful contributions. If they focus on drawing out students' love for collaboration, their classrooms will center student interactivity and engagement over performative teaching.

In this chapter, we will explore how teachers can treat students more equitably in two ways: by using a "gifted lens" and by engaging in meaningful data conversations with students.

The Gifted Lens: Fostering Asset-Based Analysis

Teachers are bombarded with tiny moments of informal data every day. In these moments, teacher beliefs are either reinforced or challenged. The lens through which teachers view their students during informal data collection shapes their treatment of students. Let's begin by exploring a five-second snapshot of what it can often feel like to take in data as a teacher.

> I'm exhausted and need more coffee. My feet are sore; I really need to buy some more comfortable dress shoes. I'm teaching this stupid main idea standard, which kids often struggle to understand, and I'm not very optimistic about

them learning in today's lesson. This lesson doesn't align with the science of reading, but the principal is coming in later to see me teach, so I need to stick to what I put in my lesson plans or I'll be on admin's radar. I spent almost an hour picking out a passage last night that I think is engaging because the curriculum isn't culturally relevant. I'll admit, I don't know it super-well because I found it around 10 p.m., but it seemed to be around my students' reading level, and hopefully my kids can relate to the passage's main character.

I'm midsentence, modeling how to pull out key information from the first page of the text to the class, when I peek up for a few seconds to scan the room. Darius and Sithu, two of my lowest readers, have their heads down. This has been the case all week. Students at the two back tables are following along, but they are all slouched and look like they'd rather stare at a brick wall than read this passage. Mario's book is nowhere to be seen, and they are doodling furiously in their notebooks. Stella and Julia are ogling each other as they play with each other's hair. Tami is telling the three students at her table a story, and they are all laughing.

The first paragraph consists of the teacher's thoughts about their own emotional state and the content of the lesson. The second paragraph pulls out data the teacher collected in a quick scan of the class and some correlated reasoning. Let's consider three ways the teacher might analyze—actively or subconsciously—what they noticed.

Deficits lens

First, let's consider the deficit lens, which focuses on students' weaknesses and struggles. Through this lens, the teacher may identify students as wrong, impulsive, disrespectful, noncompliant, or lacking readiness for success—using data to affirm preconceptions and

 DP3

stereotypes.

Assume-the-best lens

Second is the so-called assume-the-best lens, where the teacher guesses at what is happening with a student's behavior or performance. This lens, however well-intentioned, is misguided. It appears more positive than the deficit lens but hinges on limited and inferential data. With an assume-the-best lens, teachers seek to neutralize or avoid negative conclusions about a student, but student behavior or performance is still perceived as negative or insufficient. Because this avoidance limits understanding, it also limits solutions. It is likely that the dynamic will continue, the teacher will grow weary of reasoning away the behavior, and the negative perception of the behavior will return. The teacher will feel frustration or resentment and ultimately view the student similarly to the deficit lens.

The third lens is a gifted lens, which allows the teacher to see every *Gifted lens* child as a unique, exceptionally talented individual. Using a gifted lens, the teacher either examines data that's harder to immediately access or seeks that data out. Through this lens, the teacher's thinking is "If I haven't seen this kid shine, then I've got to do something differently." Figure 3.1 offers a few simplified examples of how the three lenses can shape thinking and decision making. **DP11**

As you might expect, outcomes for students can be drastically different across these three lenses. They also lead to three very different types of classrooms. Teachers who predominantly lean on a deficit lens or an assume-the-best lens create a classroom dynamic that is not only problematic and biased but also resistant to student input. When these two lenses direct a teacher's actions, classroom data (both qualitative and quantitative) often serves to marginalize students or provide evidence for a solution that is beyond the classroom or teacher.

> **Apply:** *Think of a recent interaction you had with a student that didn't go as well as you might have liked. Which lens did you use? What were some specific thoughts or behaviors that would have helped you use a gifted lens?*

As a teacher, Sonya was prudent about outsourcing classroom solutions. She focused on resolving problems directly with students in order to build trust and credibility. She continued this approach as a **EDC2** school social worker; sometimes, she would be asked to respond to a tricky conflict or behavior and found herself saying to teachers, "I don't have a secret sauce—simply the opportunity (time and space) to work something out with a kid and earn their trust." Trust can grow into a more personal understanding with each check-in, follow-up, or promise kept. Understanding students this way offers teachers the benefits of the gifted lens. Students, feeling believed in and regarded beyond their mistakes, grow more confident in their independent problem-solving abilities. Trust also returns the focus to the student; in other words, it guides actions that are responsive to the child—not just a behavior or problem.

FIGURE 3.1 • The Three Lenses

Deficit Lens (uses biased data)	Assume-the-Best Lens (uses limited or inferential data)	Gifted Lens (uses hidden data and curiosity)
Darius and Sithu are below-level readers and don't want to learn. The school psychologist and reading specialist might want to evaluate them for a learning disability.	Darius and Sithu have not been sleeping well or are having an "off" week. I spoke with their parents earlier in the week, and both mentioned that things had been rough at home.	Darius and Sithu are especially skilled at something I'm not aware of. My ELA class isn't making space for them to shine, and I need to check in with them and their other teachers to see what I'm missing.
Mario is once again unprepared for school and disinterested in improving their grade. They don't like school, their classmates, or ELA.	Mario must be going through a difficult adolescent phase. They came out to their parents on the first day of school, and ever since has been more aloof and introverted. I'll email the school counselor about helping Mario get on track in my class.	Mario seems to really enjoy creating art. I've never asked to see their drawings with any genuine interest, so I will talk to them after class.
Tami is insubordinate and struggles to follow community agreements. She doesn't care about class and is ruining the learning experience for her classmates.	Tami is a social butterfly and well-liked by her classmates. She may just need to get some socializing out of her system. If I give her a few more minutes to talk, then maybe she will quiet down.	Tami is a natural leader, able to capture the attention of her classmates, and engage them through her incredible storytelling and sense of humor. I wonder how she would respond to a class leadership opportunity. Maybe I'll see if she wants to join me for a lunch bunch so I can get an idea of how my class can play to her strengths.

By acting in concert with students, teachers broaden the data set for effective problem-solving. Using a gifted lens to mediate conflict, differentiate materials, scan the classroom for engagement, or review exit tickets makes for a classroom that pulls students in—not one that pushes them out. By nature, such individualized relational work is time-intensive and variable. In the classroom, Sonya was dogged about holding an inclusive space grounded in unconditional positive regard (Greig, 2018). There were still messy mediations, disheartening room **EDC4** scans during some of her best-planned lessons, and a few batches of exit tickets that had her thinking, "Forehead, meet desk. Desk, meet forehead." Still, students did not bear the weight of that stress on their shoulders—nor were they defined or confined by those moments. Instead, there was always another question to ask or another data point to seek. Operating with a gifted lens allowed for a mutual process of creating and gathering data.

There are also broader influences that shape how we see students, their behaviors, and their performance. Systemically, schools **EDC1** underutilize gifted programs and gifted identification practices. We pay more attention to the data that reveals student struggles than student strengths. We shouldn't throw away supports for students or ignore concerning data; rather, we must treat every child as though they have a hidden superpower that's not yet been discovered. Additionally, when we define outcome data through the narrow lens of academic achievement, we ignore the diverse nature of humanity. Success looks different for everyone. If a student is more artistic, they may show success by approaching math in a less traditional way. This is one reason that thoughtfully encouraging choice is a best practice in planning and instruction.

A Quick Note on Assessments

There are plenty of books and resources about how to analyze student assessments. Here, we intentionally divert our focus away from traditional assessments—not only because tests can be rife with bias but also because such measures, especially those leveraged by local and national policymakers, aren't the only (or primary) data point teachers should analyze. Educators who open their analysis to the richness of data around them create classrooms that better hold a child's development. Assessments, although often powerful tools that capture student learning and guide teacher actions, cannot encapsulate the scope of how we measure and monitor student growth and achievement. **DP5**

Discussing Academic Data with Students

Classrooms are where we most frequently communicate with students. As a result, we focus on developing our communication skills in service of our classrooms: clear and concise directions, a neutral tone for redirection, and so on. Though these concepts are a part of good teaching, they are aimed at one-sided communication. In education, we spend little time becoming adept at fostering meaningful dialogue with or between students and even less time learning how to solicit student feedback. When Freire (1970) warned against the "banking concept of education" (p. 72), he charged educators to pivot away from treating **DP12** students as vessels for knowledge and toward seeing them as cocreators of it.

In particular, academic data points are most equitable when they directly engage students as agents in their own learning, but there **EDC2** are pitfalls. Unfortunately, student data and shaming have long been a couple. Because many external influences determine the data we focus on and how we interpret it, teachers can also feel disempowered. Therefore, it can be challenging to resolve feelings of anxiety, shame, or confusion surrounding academic data. To counter the lows of data's emotional roller coaster, we encourage an approach such as the one Zephrah modeled at the start of this chapter. Whether through reframing the data, using the data differently, or using different data, teachers can prioritize the experiences of those most affected.

What do you say to a student who is reading multiple years below grade level yet has no formal specialized services? Too often, the answer is nothing. It can be easy to default to disingenuous words of encouragement instead of explicit, honest conversations about student progress. Here, we dive into an example of a difficult conversation between a teacher and a 9th grade student. As you will read, the teacher makes the hard but essential decision to kindly and directly explain that the student is reading below grade level. Notes in italics explain some of the best practices the teacher uses.

Teacher: Hey, Dani, thanks for stopping by after school.

Dani: No problem.

Teacher: I was hoping we could look at some of your data from the start of the school year together. Is that OK with you?

[Always ask for permission to engage in what might be a difficult conversation. If the student doesn't want to talk, find another time. It's better to have a conversation when they are ready than it is to force it.]

Dani: Sure.

Teacher: First, I'm curious what comes to your mind when I say the word *data*.

[You don't have to start with this, but kids—just like adults—are often confused about and scared of the word data. *Therefore, it can be worth taking a moment to make sure they know that data is not just about grades and test scores.]*

Dani: I guess my grades, right?

Teacher: Yep! Your grades are definitely an example of data. But there are a lot of things that are data, such as your attendance and participation in class. Letter grades are one kind of data, but sometimes grades don't represent your learning the best. Does that make sense?

Dani: I think so.

Teacher: How would you feel about looking at three kinds of your data together: your classroom participation, the essay you wrote for homework last week, and our reading diagnostic results.

Dani: OK…

Teacher: Let's start with your classroom participation. Here's my clipboard. I don't think I've shown it to you before, but it's where I keep track of student participation in class. The check mark is for attendance, and the plus symbol is for each time you shared something in our class discussions over the last three weeks. Do you notice anything?

[The teacher first has Dani do the work of analyzing the data.]

Dani: I think I have good attendance… and there seem to be a lot of plus signs in my row.

Teacher: Yeah! You haven't missed a day of school, and you've contributed in almost every class discussion we've had. How do you feel about our classroom discussions?

[Notice that the teacher doesn't ask, "Do you like our discussions?" or "Do you like to talk?" Those are leading questions. Asking about Dani's feelings maintains an inquiry stance and doesn't make assumptions.]

Dani: I don't know. I don't really like to talk in front of everyone. I like when we get to talk in groups.

Teacher: That's really helpful for me to know. I'll do my best to include more small-group discussion time. I remember on Monday in class, that point you brought up about the book's theme was really thoughtful! And it seemed like your classmates felt the same way because a lot of discussion happened after you said that. I really appreciate the way you open up in groups, and I'm sure your classmates do, too.

[The teacher now has further direction to guide upcoming lesson planning and takes the opportunity to genuinely praise Dani for one of her assets with a specific example, helping to build trust and validation of real efforts.]

Dani: Thanks!

Teacher: I'm excited to be with you in class tomorrow when we pick it back up! Before we look at your essay, I wanted to ask, could you share with me how you feel about writing?

Dani: [looks down] I don't know.

Teacher: Is writing something you feel confident about?

[The teacher shifts to an easier question because of Dani's body language.]

Dani: Not really.

Teacher: That's OK. That's why you're in school: to improve your reading and writing skills. And I'm absolutely here to help.

Dani: [still looking down, not saying anything]

Teacher: How do you feel about writing in Spanish?

Dani: [looks up] Is that an option?

Teacher: Absolutely! Probably not for every assignment; otherwise I won't have a chance to give you feedback on your English writing skills, but if you want to write in Spanish more often, that works for me. You can even do both—a mix of Spanish and English—if you want.

Dani: Alright… I don't like what I wrote in the essay. I sorta hate writing.

Teacher: I absolutely detested writing when I was your age, but I had this great teacher in 9th grade who showed me how to write and now I love it. That's actually one of the reasons I became a teacher. Would you be willing to rewrite your essay for me? And can you try to write it in English, but anywhere you get stuck, you can write in Spanish. How does that sound?

Dani: OK. I kinda like that.

Teacher: Great! So, this might sound like a weird question, but I'm curious if any of your previous teachers have ever talked to you about your reading level?

Dani: Not much. I mean, Ms. Barber told me I was reading at a high school level even though I was only in 6th grade.

Teacher: OK, and did you feel like the reading diagnostic we took a few weeks ago was something you did your best on?

Dani: Yeah. It was really hard, though.

Teacher: Yes, diagnostics are meant to be pretty challenging. A lot of students struggled with it, but I appreciate you putting your best effort forward and showing me what you know. I noticed your hard work. So, Dani, I'm here to support you, and I really aim to be honest with my students so we can work for the most growth possible while we're together. We all have strengths where we shine and growth areas to work on. From what I've seen so far, you have a lot of strengths, like your attendance, participation, and thoughtful additions to small-group discussions. And your courage to talk to your group so openly! It's clear that you like books and want to become a better reader and writer. So for those things, it's awesome to see where you're at. Something we might work on this year is your reading, though. According to the results of the diagnostic test, you're reading lower than where we aim for most 9th graders to be. This is just one test, but it works on levels, and if you were to move three levels this school year, it could really change how you've been feeling about your work.

[Note the qualifier "this is just one test" as an acknowledgment that one assessment—especially one that produces a reading level— likely isn't a perfect measure.]

DP2

Dani: [looking down] I don't know.

Teacher: Dani, from what I've seen in just the first few weeks of school, you're going to grow immensely this year. You can get your score up a *lot* if you're willing to put the effort in. It will take extra work, but I'll help. We can do this together. I've taught so many students who scored similarly on this diagnostic, and within a year or two, they were reading on or above grade level. It won't always be easy, but I am saying it is definitely possible.

Dani: [after a moment] OK.

Teacher: How about you take some time to process. I know I threw a lot at you just now, so let's check back in later this week.

[Giving Dani space to process is really important. The teacher must remember to reconnect with Dani—and probably Dani's family— later in the week and can stay inquisitive about Dani's feelings. Dani will likely need a lot of praise and encouragement over the next few weeks to stay invested in the class. She will also need guidance on some specific ways to grow: extra assignments, after-school meetings, or a peer tutor could be options. However, Dani should be in the driver's seat, while the teacher's guidance should encourage challenging yet realistic growth.]

Let's unpack just a few of the successes in this student data conversation. First, without intentional data collection, the teacher would not have a sense of Dani's performance or be able to engage in this conversation. Showing Dani multiple data points was key to clarifying that she brings many strengths into the classroom *and* that there is a concern. Additionally, data was not wielded as an accountability tool but shared as a measure for feedback. To further this dynamic, the teacher let Dani take the lead, even though there was reticence to engage in some aspects of the conversation. Probing for Dani's current feelings about academic data allowed the teacher to calibrate the accessibility of the conversation in the moment. That empowered Dani not only to draw conclusions from the data but also to feel agency in how it could be used moving forward. The teacher was able to honestly—and specifically—discuss Dani's reading level without missing opportunities to let her know her teacher would be an encouraging, supportive partner in that growth.

It's tempting to cushion language to students about their academic status. Having a conversation with a child who is reading significantly behind grade level can be intimidating and heavy. Some teachers may be concerned about hurting a student's feelings or upsetting family members. Some may project feelings of guilt and anger at systemic factors in ways that burden the dialogue or path to progress. However, telling an 11th grader who is reading at a 3rd grade level that they can go to medical school without having a genuine conversation about their reading skills simply does a disservice to that student. It's disrespectful and relies on an expectation that systems beyond the classroom will be similarly condescending (and exclusionary) in deciding that this kind of conversation does not matter for the student.

You should also invite families into these data conversations. Conversations about student data with family members are just as important as conversations with students. Although this book doesn't have space to fully address how to collaborate with families, they are foundational to our work with students. Tending to a clear, supportive connection with a student's support system before, during, and after tough conversations can shift outcomes significantly. Students' families will have their own unique orientations to data, and it may help you better support students if you learn about their family members' beliefs and hopes for them.

Apply: *How do conversations with students who are behind currently sound in your classroom, office, or special education meetings? What language can help you push candor, transparency, and accessibility while also asserting unconditional positive regard, supportiveness, and dignity?*

Conclusion: Beyond the Classroom

Holding space for students and families is a critical responsibility for teachers and school leaders. We must initiate honest conversations about student progress that offer students and families meaningful data and an understanding of resources available to them. We must also ensure that students know and feel, through the genuine care of a trusting adult, that they are not defined by a number, statistic, or score. The person must always come first. If we can model and embody that mindset—best enacted through a gifted lens and in our collaborative, attentive conversations with students—then students will take their positive self-concept beyond the classroom and into all aspects of their lives.

4

Student Well-Being: Healing-Centered Engagement, Restorative Practices, and Tracking Critical Incidents

Listen to me, now. I say I been wrong, son.
That I been doing to you what the rest of the world been doing to you.

—Lorraine Hansberry, *A Raisin in the Sun*

I Think She Wants an Apology

When I (Sonya) heard that Camila had a "moment" in Ms. Jay's math class, I was worried. Like many middle schoolers, Camila was a classic M&Ms kind of kid: soft on the inside, hard shell on the outside. Depending on whom you asked, she could be either warm and friendly or cold and defiant. I grew to know her well through our daily routine of having lunch in my office. I had seen Camila's growth, particularly over the past year. She had been gradually turning toward trusting relationships with her teachers.

Ms. Jay was an experienced math teacher, but she was new to our school. I didn't know much about her in-the-moment response to students, but she seemed to be a strong relationship-builder and generally well-liked by kids. However, a classroom situation can uncover a teacher's underlying biases, fears, or drive to feel safe by feeling in control, and a teacher's needs don't always pair well with a student's needs during those moments.

As a school social worker and administrator, I've found that the relationship between a teacher and student is one of the most important data points in my work. Uncovering and repairing conflict between teachers and students strengthens our school community and creates emotional safety for everyone.

At the end of the day, I stopped by Ms. Jay's room. She explained that Camila had been "on a roll" during a class discussion when another student, Luca, interrupted her. There was some back-and-forth between the students, and a few moments later, Ms. Jay called on Luca again, even though Camila also had her hand raised. Camila, likely feeling sad, silenced, and hurt (amplified by the developmental experience of middle school), yelled at Luca, yelled at Ms. Jay, and then walked out of class, slamming the door behind her.

Ms. Jay shared, "I realized right away that I should have called on at least a couple of other students before I returned to Luca. And I should have returned to our discussion agreements, stopped Luca when he interrupted Camila, or checked back in on Camila to make sure she was OK and had shared what she wanted to share. Camila didn't handle the situation well, but neither did I."

Ms. Jay understood. She acknowledged how she could have done better. She also knew that Camila probably felt betrayed, even if Ms. Jay thought the experience was trivial and didn't fit into a rational adult schema. She simply had to understand what sense the student made of the problem.

Knowing she was empathetically attuned to the situation and student, I celebrated the trust she'd clearly gained to even be in this situation. I shared my confidence that their trust was still intact, even if it felt dinged. There was a clear path to strengthening their relationship and for Ms. Jay to model restorative communication. Instead of trying to resolve the situation for her, I asked, "How do you think you'll follow up?"

"I think she wants an apology from me."

I held my breath, waiting to see where she might go.

"That's going to be hard for me. We don't really do apologies in my family. I don't really do apologies."

I left Ms. Jay's classroom feeling confident about what would come next but also impressed by her vulnerability and grateful for her insight. Many of us inherit the idea that adults shouldn't apologize. Particularly to kids. Nevertheless, all educators inevitably make mistakes that affect students—in the classroom, at dismissal, while covering a class, or when we're tired or hungry or stressed. As it often goes, kids learn and feel a lot from what we show (or don't show) them.

All educators make mistakes

The next morning, Ms. Jay showed Camila that she was worth an apology—a good one. The kind that's said out loud. The kind that leaves someone feeling seen, heard, and irreplaceable in the space you share. An apology that invites a plan for a better try next time and maybe even a good laugh. An interaction that quickly boosts both the teacher and student's well-being.

Boost the Ss' & Ts' well being

Sure enough, Camila returned to Ms. Jay's class even more invested and engaged. She seemed determined to meet Ms. Jay where Ms. Jay

> met her—just beyond the comfort zone. Although their relationship wasn't perfect, about a month later, Camila started politely skipping out on lunches in my office to hang out in Ms. Jay's classroom.
> I don't have a more reliable measure of success than that.

Relationships are the driver of Ss' well-being

Leaders know that relationships are critical to the functioning of a school because they are a key driver of students' well-being. We can't have happy, thriving students who are ready to learn without trusting relationships and clear pathways to resolving conflicts.

With that in mind, how do you measure or evaluate student well-being? How can we improve data practices to create safer, more equitable schools for students? School leaders can be respectful and responsible stewards of student well-being by leaning on the stories that students, families, and staff offer as critical data points. The right data will help leaders navigate and respond to conflict. When school staff approach conflict realistically—as a naturally occurring event in human relationships rather than misbehavior—they unlock more opportunities for solutions. Often, these kinds of solutions are more inclusive of students and, thus, more productive.

From Trauma to Healing-Centered Engagement

We begin with a caution. Sometimes, the very attempt to operationalize relationships can detract from students' most human qualities. To complicate matters, the personal context or sensitive information that students or families share with us can (and should) feel sacred—worthy of protection and privacy.

DP1 Not every student data point should be shared with everyone. Leaders can gather and share student data in ethical ways. For instance, a student might confide in a leader that there was a death in their family. That leader's first reaction might be to inform all the teachers, wanting them to be sensitive to the student's needs. However, some teachers may respond better than others. In her role, Sonya is regularly approached by teachers who seek out student data that might explain

why a student hasn't turned in homework or hasn't otherwise met expectations. She doesn't always share that information, sometimes because it feels like a violation of privacy and sometimes because she is not confident that sharing details of a student's home life will necessarily improve the teacher's ability to work with the student.

One of the most misused approaches to understanding students' social-emotional data is a dependence on a trauma lens. The seminal ACEs (adverse childhood experiences) study in the 1990s codified trauma as a key data point about students (Centers for Disease Control and Prevention, 2020). However, the study was conducted with a participant pool of predominantly White, college-educated participants over the age of 60, which is not representative of the classrooms in which most educators work. Furthermore, an intense focus on trauma can activate a deficit-based approach to how we engage students.

Trauma lens can lead to deficit approach

As trauma made the rounds on professional development agendas, we somehow shifted from asking how our classrooms function in relation to certain students' experiences to planning for how certain students might function in our classrooms. Data around trauma can exacerbate bias, disconnecting educators from students by boiling students down to a single experience. Some schools even took it upon themselves to survey for trauma without considering the impact of probing for such sensitive information or having the resources to adequately address it. Maybe because of its roots in healthcare, the language around trauma-informed schools evolved to include terms of diagnosis and assumption. Suddenly, it seemed like we were training teachers to anticipate the behavioral and academic capacities of students who most likely experienced trauma. These approaches—promoting an overreliance on a limited data set and encouraging inferential analysis—are problematic for our work as school-based data practitioners.

 DP1

 DP3

 DP11

Understanding how traumatic experiences can affect our minds and bodies is incredibly relevant to our work. Trauma-informed care concepts are integral to education, especially as they improve our ability to create learning environments that feel safe. However, in supporting individual students, we must be attuned to what they tell us (or show us) works. Student-informed care is trauma-informed care, but the reverse is not always true. The approaches and tools offered in this chapter help school leaders find a balance between theory and practice when it comes to putting student well-being first.

Shawn Ginwright (2018), professor of education in the department of Africana studies and senior research associate at San Francisco State University, offers a valuable reframing of trauma-informed care: healing-centered engagement (HCE). Instead of solely focusing on trauma, HCE is an approach that "highlights the ways in which trauma and healing are experienced collectively" (para. 10). A healing-centered classroom fosters a culture of well-being for students and deemphasizes students' individual traumatic histories. Figure 4.1 shows the four key elements of HCE that help leaders center student well-being and build an equitable data culture in schools.

healing- centered engagement

HCE shifts trauma out of the lead role and challenges the pathologizing or deterministic messaging within some trauma-focused frameworks. It also demands acknowledgment of systemic influences that contribute to the environmental stressors students experience. For Sonya, this explicit orientation to the systemic was the most compelling in her reflections as an educator. It became glaringly apparent how few academic or professional spaces discussed the injustices enacted by school policies or positioned school systems as a perpetuator of multiple ACEs. To ignore this connection and focus so rigidly on the relationship between a student, a traumatic event, and brain-based behaviors feels like an action of complicity.

> **Apply:** *Which elements of HCE resonate with you the most? Which challenge you the most?*

Informal Data About Student Feelings

Daily data collection on how Ss are feeling

Educators need informal systems that gather information about how students are feeling each day. Those systems help ensure we don't neglect the quiet student in the back of the room or ignore the child who comes to school with a cloud over their head. Making space for interpersonal connections can make the difference between a child feeling supported and a child feeling sidelined or mined for data.

Data that empowers Ss

Leaders should break away from trauma-centered data and shift toward data that empowers students to share their stories. What is the first data point about student well-being we gather each morning?

FIGURE 4.1 • Four Key Elements of Healing-Centered Engagement

Explicitly political rather than clinical

Under trauma-focused approaches, schools often distance themselves from their complicity in perpetuating student trauma. This distancing is at best akin to silent colorblindness; at worst, it is a form of gaslighting the very families schools claim to serve. HCE focuses on maximizing benefit for participants and rejects the idea that trauma only takes place *outside* schools. Using HCE, data gathering focuses on the traumatizing practices taking place *inside* our schools. Schools traumatize students through metal detectors, punitive disciplinary approaches, and a lack of mental health support. Therefore, schools can't be apolitical, nor can they be seen as a community savior. Schools are just as much a part of the systemic problem.

"Communities and individuals who experience trauma are agents in restoring their own well-being" (Ginwright, 2018, para. 13), so our data practices must be collaborative. Centering trauma also often means taking a clinical, symptoms-oriented approach, which can cause educators to see students as victims rather than agents of their own healing. HCE focuses on bringing purpose, power, and control to people.

Culturally grounded; Views healing as a restoration of identity

Where an overemphasis on trauma might see students more clinically as patients or victims, HCE elevates the importance of individuals' unique culture and identity. Students have rich identities that can go ignored if they are only defined by their trauma. Restoring well-being also means fostering a sense of belonging and community. Youth of color especially benefit from seeing a shared racial and ethnic identity. Our data-gathering practices must therefore be less extractive and more collaborative. Students should be the ones telling us how their trauma shows up for them; we should not be telling them what trauma has done or will do to them.

Asset-driven; Focused on desired well-being rather than symptoms of suppression

Our students are more than their trauma. They are multifaceted and complex individuals—not single data points—who know themselves better than we ever will. An asset-driven approach to healing validates and builds on students' existing positive traits, their knowledge and skills, and their curiosity and self-awareness. Trauma-driven practices focus on "symptom suppression" where educators operate with the goal of stopping the symptoms of trauma. HCE focuses on the larger aim of healing instead of just correcting or changing a single negative manifestation of trauma. HCE is also more participatory and inquisitive. When we seek out data about our students, HCE directs us to work with students, listening to their experiences and needs. We must stay inquisitive and recognize that data gives us clues, not answers.

Supports adult providers with their own healing

HCE places educators and practitioners in the healing work. Educators bring their own identities, feelings, healing needs, first- and second-hand traumas, and experience. Data practices that focus on student well-being can't harm teachers. Our approach can't just be good for kids; it must also work for adults. Everyone in the school community deserves to heal.

Source: Content derived from "The Future of Healing: Shifting from Trauma Informed Care to Healing Centered Engagement" by S. Ginwright, 2018. Used with permission.

 DP1

 EDC1

 EDC2

 EDC2

 EDC3

 EDC3

 DP11

 EDC1

 DP12

Is it their attendance? Their emotional state as we meet them in the schoolyard or as they arrive to the classroom? Most leaders know how important this information can be, but it's usually collected in a flurry. Distracted and frazzled, educators often don't leverage some of the simplest and most accessible forms of informal data about student well-being. Here are some ways you can strengthen data collection on student well-being at the start of the day.

School Entry Pulse Check

Morning entry is a unique time of day when school leaders can connect with students. If you don't already, you should attempt to greet every child by name as they enter the building. If you notice a student isn't having a good morning, offer their name to the counselor for a check-in or, better yet, check in with them before their first class begins. Once this ritual is established, you can also begin to use what you notice during morning entry to build rapport each day. Although many leaders engage in this practice, few view morning entry as a simple and

DP6 powerful form of data collection.

Check-In, Check-Out

For students who consistently have tough days, a check-in, check-out system offers the opportunity to connect with a trusted adult of their choosing. The school counselor or social worker can be the check-in person for any students who don't yet have an adult with whom they feel comfortable working. School leaders should also keep a list of those students handy either formally or informally. Every student should be able to identify at least one adult in the building they'd trust enough for a check-in. If they say they don't care who it is or that there's no one, the check-in, check-out system is even more important to implement.

At the Classroom Door

Similar to morning entry, how students show up to a classroom can communicate a lot about how their day is going. Be intentional about not only how you want to structure these interactions but also how students might want to share their thoughts and feelings. Younger students might have a "choose your greeting" menu, whereas quick small-talk exchanges with older students might better meet their needs. Teachers need to be trusted in these moments to direct students to counselors or take a time-out with a student before class starts.

Some of the most effective teachers will ask a student to hang out with them outside the class for a few minutes while other students engage in an independent opening activity. That extra few minutes in the hall creates a safer, less public space for data gathering. Although these encounters are brief, they still have value. Setting the expectation that kids don't enter the learning environment if they aren't ready to learn requires a lot of training for teachers, but it prevents larger issues from boiling over. It's much easier for a teacher to gather data one-on-one with a student than it is to absorb data about every student during the lesson.

Zones of Regulation

The zones of regulation (Kuypers, 2019) refer to four different feeling categories that are organized by color: blue for feeling sad or tired, green for feeling happy or calm, yellow for feeling worried or anxious, and red for feeling angry or overexcited. This self-reporting system for emotional data collection helps students build emotional intelligence by talking about their feelings—something students, especially male students, are socialized to avoid (Plank, 2019)—and build empathy by listening to others share. It also helps teachers easily gather data from students about their well-being. Teachers should model the optional process before expecting students to use the tool proficiently. They share how they are feeling, which zone they are in, and why they're in that zone. This allows everyone to talk about how they are feeling at the start of the day, which sets teachers and students up for higher levels of empathy.

It can sometimes feel like a distraction from learning, but the students who need these brief supports will only be more distracted if we ignore their social-emotional well-being. High school teachers often find it hard to justify taking time for even short interactions that generate data from students about their well-being. Indeed, a 50-minute instructional block often feels too short to "lose" even 5–10 minutes, yet these check-ins build an essential foundation. They are good for students because they build self-awareness and empathy, and they are good for educators because they provide invaluable data about students' feelings and their readiness to learn.

School leaders must protect this time, whether it's daily morning meetings, proactive restorative circles, or impromptu conferences. They must explicitly say that community building around students' feelings and day-to-day experiences are necessary for learning. When leaders share this priority with their leadership teams, teachers, and **EDC4** staff, they should clarify that this information matters just as much as, and sometimes more than, much of the other data we gather. School leaders can support teachers in becoming comfortable with gathering this kind of data skillfully, authentically, and sustainably.

Informal data collection only takes us so far. We need data approaches that don't just help us tap into students' emotional and experiential well-being; we also need data approaches that help us address conflict and repair relationships.

> **Apply:** *What other kinds of informal data do you gather throughout the day?*

Restorative Practices and Tracking Critical Incidents

School discipline systems can pull in an immense amount of data that can be tricky to use. There are more narrative chunks of information such as discipline referrals and mediation logs, and there's smaller bits of information such as merit and demerit data or suspension and detention stats. This data often results in school staff following up for more information, which is a good instinct; it is a response to the potential for **DP2** bias and a recognition that these data points are fluid. However, unless they are baked into a larger system focused on student well-being and healing, our discipline systems too often exhaust adults and fail to repair harm.

Restorative practices (RP) is an approach that mitigates and resolves conflict with others in a manner that strengthens relationships and social connections. It pulls from Indigenous Māori traditions and breaks from punitive measures by addressing harm through increased human connection (Wachtel, 2016). In addition, RP is a beneficial frame **EDC2** work for building an equitable data culture in schools since it centers collaboration with others by elevating student stories and staying inquisitive. The social discipline window (Figure 4.2), a key grounding concept within RP, shows how our interactions with students should include high control (limit-setting) and high support (encouragement). **EDC3**

FIGURE 4.2 • Social Discipline Window

TO punitive authoritarian	**WITH** restorative authoritative
NOT neglectful irresponsible	**FOR** permissive paternalistic

control (limit-setting, discipline) — LOW to HIGH (vertical axis)

support (encouragement, nurture) — LOW to HIGH (horizontal axis)

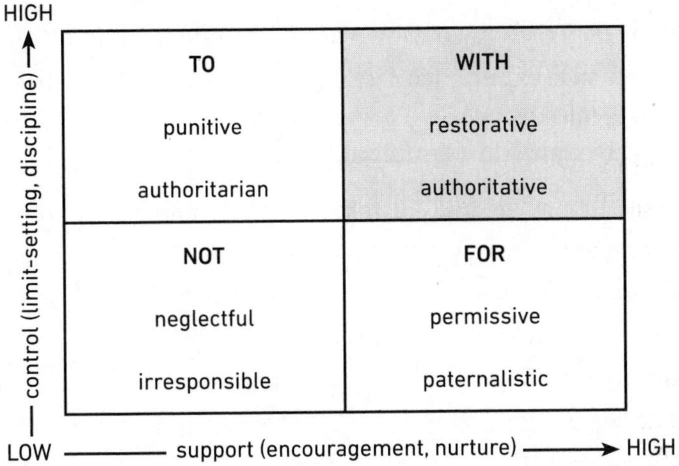

Source: From "Defining Restorative" by T. Wachtel, 2016, www.iirp.edu/restorative-practices/defining-restorative. Copyright 2016 by the International Institute for Restorative Practices. Used with permission.

Restorative practices offers an approach to data gathering and analysis that breaks traditional power dynamics; it establishes the adult as the individual in control, but it centers students and their experiences by having them do most of the work. In a restorative conversation, the adult asks questions, and the student answers them. In a restorative **EDC3** conference for students, the students do most of the talking with one another and share their experiences. Adults invite students to share **EDC3** their insights, stories, and experiences by asking open-ended, restorative questions such as "What have you been thinking about since this happened?" or "What do you think you can do to make things right?" Whereas more traditional or punitive approaches to discipline solicit a single story about conflict and churn out a quick consequence, RP invites more storytelling, examines the intersections of our stories, and

[handwritten note in right margin: " Restorative data gathering"]*

EDC2

connect us to a bigger picture of belonging. This kind of qualitative data exchange is critical to develop more realistic views of others and help us uncover more meaningful solutions.

A student calls another student a homophobic slur during gym class. An algebra teacher tells a student who is Vietnamese that she's surprised he's not better at math. A student rips off a Muslim girl's hijab in a busy hallway. An unfathomable number of racist words and actions go unnoticed by school personnel every day. Students can be bullied, harassed, sexualized, and discriminated against without staff knowing. Sometimes, it may even be our own staff who cause harm or offense. We know students can experience feelings of pain or sadness that directly impede their ability to learn.

Even when incidents are reported, many go unaddressed. Deans or administrators who respond first to incidents often don't have the immediate capacity, resources, or training to respond comprehensively when a student has experienced something emotionally or physically distressing. School climate leaders are stretched thin and expected to focus primarily on the incidents that are tracked—an ongoing reminder that the data we gather dictates our day-to-day behavior as school leaders. Many systems for reporting incidents set the implicit or explicit bar that if it's not a physical fight or if a teacher isn't cursed out, then it's not big enough to warrant an incident report.

The devastating impact of daily racism cannot be ignored just because it seems invisible for some. How can school leaders bring these concerns to light? At one school in Colorado, the mostly White leadership team's biggest equity challenge was what they didn't know. As the principal described, "Microaggressions were happening, and we had no clue. We were basically out to lunch." She knew her team couldn't understand the student experience without figuring out what was happening behind the scenes. Consequently, the leadership team built an open-access Google Form for students to share critical incidents with staff. They defined a *critical incident* as follows:

> A system or an interaction that can affect anyone and cause harm, which is inherently oppressive (the experience of harm, even if not intended). This must be repaired through self-awareness about bias, which breaks and disrupts oppressive systems (local and historical). It can be repaired through

an intentional restorative process that requires reflection to create a resolution that results in improved understanding, ultimately leading to equity and a sense of belonging to the community.

They also offered more student-friendly language for a student-facing definition:

A critical incident is a moment or time when I have felt "othered"—like I didn't belong—and it felt harmful and damaging to my identity. In this moment, I felt like there was no solution and no way to repair the relationship because I felt powerless.

The leadership team first normed around the belief that most incidents within their school community were not rooted in hate. In the rare case that an incident stemmed from hate and discrimination, they would follow a more intensive process. Deans continued to focus on handling immediate urgent issues, but the principal and her equity team focused on monitoring and responding to the critical incident tracker. As they gathered data throughout the day or week, they could flag which incidents needed a quicker follow-up and who might be the best person to reach out to the people involved.

Most of the follow-up conversations involved some kind of mediation. The team's follow-up was simple. They asked, "What do you need to feel good about coming back to our community?" They also recognized how individual those needs can be. Surprisingly, most of the incidents were reconciled relatively quickly. In many cases, the individual who had caused harm did so without realizing the damage they had done and was genuinely apologetic, and the harmed student was often forgiving and understanding. As needed, the team also used logical consequences to help repair harm. By acknowledging and responding to the harm that would normally sit with students and undermine connectedness, the school provided students with an opportunity for healing.

This taught students valuable lessons about empathy, community, and relational awareness. In engaging in these restorative conversations, the adults were simultaneously validating students' experiences and modeling problem-solving behavior. They built credibility with the student body because they followed up on every incident that was reported. As a team, they were able to recognize the types of challenges students experienced in their community when it came to equity. Figure 4.3 shows the content of the form used to gather and track critical incidents at this school.

FIGURE 4.3 • Critical Incidents Tracker

SPEAK UP! Against language or actions that harm members of our community 2021–22

At [our school]: We don't act or use language of any kind that harms or belittles any member of our community regardless of intent. In order to ensure that our community is safe and supportive of EVERYONE, please SPEAK UP and report language (verbal, non-verbal) or actions that harm or belittle a member of our community.

(General Questions)

• Email address:
• Is this an incident that poses an immediate threat to the safety of someone in our community? Yes / No
• What is your role in the community? Student / Staff or Community Member

(Student - Part A)

• What type of incident occurred?
– Verbal communication / Non-verbal / Physical / Hard-copy (writing on paper, walls, etc.) / Soft copy (social media, email, etc.) / Other
• When did the incident occur? (Do your best to estimate if it didn't happen recently and you don't know the date)
– Date
• Where did the incident occur?
– Classroom / Hallway during class / Hallways during passing period / Lunch or Break / Bathroom / Before school / After school / Social media / Don't know where / Other
• What was your role?
– Survivor (the target of the racial or identity-based language) / Upstander (you witnessed the incident and intervened to stop it and stand up for the shared values of our community) / Bystander (you witnessed the incident but did not or were not able to intervene) / Offender (you caused the harm using racial or identity-based language) / Was not present but heard about the event

(Student - Part B: Survivor, Upstander, Bystander, Heard about the event)

• If you were not the survivor/target of this incident, what is their name?
• What is the name of the person responsible for words or actions that had a harmful impact on you or others?
• Describe what happened.
• Who else witnessed the incident as an upstander or bystander?
• What other context (background) information can you provide about the people involved in this incident?
• What do you believe would help our community move forward from this incident? Would you like an individual check-in?

(Student - Part B: Offender (self report)) • Describe what happened
(Staff) • Who is involved in this incident and what are their roles? • Describe this incident (what did you see, hear). • If not yet stated, who were witnesses to this incident (name as many people, staff included, that witnessed it). • What led up to this incident? • What were your actions?
• What do you believe would help our community move forward from this incident? Would you like an individual check-in? (Note: you can request that you would not like any follow-up and are reporting to have this on the record.)

Source: Used with permission from the Denver School of Science and Technology, Denver, Colorado.

Conclusion: Protecting Well-Being

Supporting students' well-being can be an overwhelming responsibility. How do we prevent and respond to harms across an entire school in ways that feel meaningful to each student? That challenge is not made any less daunting when the morning starts off with news of pandemic-related stressors, ism-fueled hate, personal tragedy, or violence in our community. It can be hard to know how to calibrate our support and create space for healing.

School leaders must invest time and energy in building a school culture that doesn't make student well-being sound like a reductionist or corny ideal. There are no tools more meaningful or effective at promoting student well-being than healthy, consistent, validating, and trusting relationships. Our data practices must place those relationships at the heart of our work—whether rooted in informal interactions or structured systems in which students feel safe to speak about harm in their school community. As we strengthen our relationships with students, the data they bring to us will expand and deepen, empowering us to better meet their needs.

5

Teacher Selection: Recruitment, Hiring, and Evaluation

It is urgent that we drum up more support in this country for public schools that are popular, effective, democratic, and happy and whose teachers are well paid, well trained, and in constant development.

—Paulo Freire (2005)

The "Angry Black Teacher"

For six years, Beverly Powell was one of only two Black teachers in her high school. She was also the only person of color on the instructional leadership team. An immigrant, driven by the echoing sounds of her parents saying, "You must work twice as hard to get half as much," Beverly stayed up late to prepare lessons and plan professional development for her team, despite her husband and daughter asking her to put her work aside.

Beverly brought confidence, passion, and vision to her work. She was a strong teacher but not the best in the school, and she was a strong leader but not the best in the school. In short, Beverly was not "extraordinary."

Beverly was often perceived as the "angry Black woman" by teachers and administrators alike. Her communication style was called "direct and abrasive," but it was not unlike that of her White women colleagues who had working-class upbringings. Whereas the White women were seen as assertive and sarcastic, Beverly was seen as rude and overbearing. As her coach, I (Andrew) admit that I had to check myself regularly during our coaching conversations. I remember getting red in the face when she

94

flatly rejected one of my coaching suggestions in front of a colleague whom I was training. My embarrassment in that moment heightened my awareness that our cultural differences required me to reframe and restrategize how we could connect with each other. As soon as I saw her passion and confidence, as well as the unique perspective she brought to our work together, I began to look forward to our conversations. They were spontaneous, challenging, and even fun.

Beverly brought many assets to her school—namely, her perspectives as a person of color, the only Black woman on staff, and an immigrant in a school serving a large population of first- and second-generation immigrant children. She was also a powerhouse relationship-builder in the classroom. Nevertheless, her strengths weren't what her school valued, based on the way administration spoke about "ideal" teaching, the questions they asked in teacher interviews, and the evaluation scores they gave Beverly.

Eventually, Beverly left the school. She loved her students and their families, along with most of her colleagues, but she could not see a path to continued professional opportunities and was tired of the constant skepticism and critique. She simply couldn't win within a system that didn't value what she brought to work every day.

Ibram X. Kendi (2019) writes, "One of the fundamental values of racism to White people is that it makes success attainable for even unexceptional Whites, while success, even moderate success, is usually reserved for extraordinary Black people" (p. 93). Beverly wasn't extraordinary; she was a good teacher and leader—but not a perfect one. She also refused to completely assimilate into the White dominant culture of her school. She chose to leave because of the lack of understanding and support she received from fellow staff.

Teacher quality is one of the most important predictors of student success (Goldhaber, 2016). When recruiting, hiring, and evaluating teachers, school leaders must determine what *quality* means. What data are leaders gathering to vet for high-quality candidates? What data will reveal the most qualified teachers? What other factors—beyond traditional content and pedagogical knowledge—are important for building a diverse, inclusive school community?

This chapter describes how school leaders can use EDC as a framework during teacher selection and evaluation to ensure that antiracist teachers are working with students every day. To that end, we can leverage EDC to hire and retain more teachers of color and White teachers who are committed to antiracist work.

A note before we continue: school leaders rarely have complete control over recruitment, hiring, and evaluation. These processes are steeped in restrictions (some reasonable and some not) from federal and state laws. Because the legal system conflates considering diversity with "reverse racism," any decisions made by race are, for the most part, strictly forbidden. Travis J. Bristol, who has extensively researched a diverse teaching workforce, highlights the irony: "Not everyone believes we should preference race in our attempt to recruit teachers of color" (personal communication, November 9, 2020).

It is a delicate dance. In the fight to balance a racially imbalanced teacher pipeline, you are barred from explicitly using race as a hiring criterion. However, even though leaders cannot hire teachers explicitly based on race, they can hire based on *antiracism*, which may be the next best thing.

The Need for Teachers of Color

In one rural school in the South, Michael discovered a concerning data point. In a school where 95 percent of students were Black and 100 percent of students were experiencing poverty, there were just two Black male teachers in the school. When he approached the Black male principal to discuss how he could be of help to the school, he was met with a disappointing surprise. The principal didn't want to help the two educators thrive; he wanted to push them out and replace them with "better" teachers. This was a clear case of a school leader—a man of color—ignoring a key data point and in need of examining his own mindset.

Educator diversity results in positive outcomes for students (Mota-medi & Stevens, 2018). Teachers of color often have higher expectations for, build more trusting relationships with, provide culturally relevant learning opportunities for, and advocate for the needs of students of color (Carver-Thomas, 2018). In addition, White teachers benefit from having colleagues of color. There's often more assistance with navigating unfamiliar cultural territory and designing culturally sustaining pedagogy when there is a diverse group of teachers in a school (Strauss, 2015). It is essential for all students to see reflections of themselves and understand the role intersectionality plays in defining who someone believes themselves to be and how they view the world. Having a teacher who appreciates and validates, for example, their language, culture, ethnicity, or religion is incredibly important for students' overall well-being and the comfort they feel in school.

Unfortunately, Black teachers tend to have high turnover rates driven by challenging working conditions and a dearth of mentoring opportunities (Carver-Thomas, 2018). Black male teachers in particular are more likely to experience "hypersurveillance" from administrators and are more often expected to comply with a single pedagogical approach, such as a scripted curriculum (Strauss, 2015). Many teachers of color feel isolated when there aren't other teachers in the school who look like them. Teachers of color also typically take on additional emotional labor; their enhanced ability to relate to students of color often translates to the expectation that they will do so without a reduction in other responsibilities. There is often an added emotional tax for teachers of color, especially in schools that don't have an antiracist culture. All of this is reflected in challenging retention data.

> **Apply:** *What are the retention rates of teachers of color in your school or district? Is anyone keeping track of why teachers of color (specifically) are leaving?*

Selection Committee Data

The first step in hiring antiracist teachers is assembling a selection team or committee. School leaders can gather a quick data snapshot using four *yes* or *no* questions related to demographics, mindsets, and the makeup of the selection team: **EDC1**

- Does the diversity (race, gender, and other identity markers) of the team reflect the diversity you are seeking in the school?
- Are teachers and school community members, including students and parents, on the team?
- Has the team spent sufficient time learning about bias in hiring?
- Have team members shared their own mindsets and beliefs about what makes a high-quality teacher?

If you answered *yes* to all these questions, great! If you answered *no*, explore what would move you to a *yes*.

After assembling the selection team, identify the specific selection criteria you're looking for in candidates. Those criteria will be the core data your team should gather throughout the process. Here are a few examples of criteria you might want to include:

- Candidate centers social-emotional, restorative, and/or healing-centered support over strict discipline strategies or "running a tight ship."
- Candidate conveys evidence of culturally competent teaching (prioritized over content knowledge).
- Candidate demonstrates belief in Black excellence and brings a gifted lens to their interactions with students.
- Candidate shows a track record of learning and growth.
- Candidate can comfortably speak about how their identities (especially race and gender) manifest in their teaching.
- Candidate will make the staff more diverse through identity, culture, and experiences.

The mindsets and worldviews of the selection committee will dictate the degree to which bias creeps into the process. Having open conversations as a team up front will mitigate biases, align hiring practices with the school's equity focus, and allow for a more diverse candidate pool. For example, the team might discuss questions such as the following:

- Why does teacher selection matter?
- What has been the equity stance of teachers in our school in the past?
- What does teacher turnover at our school currently look like? Are those who are staying representative of the mindsets we are looking to build?
- As the selection team, what biases might we bring to the selection process?
- In what ways has our teacher selection process resulted in less teacher diversity in the past?
- What is the power structure on our selection team? Will that result in equitable decision making? Who will ask questions? Who will conduct the outreach or be the point person for candidates?

Examining the team's mindsets and goals while planning for recruitment and hiring can help illuminate the ways in which the team's biases and misaligned beliefs may be hindering the actual efforts to increase diversity. You might find that certain power dynamics require a major **EDC4** disruption to the structure of the selection team. A mostly male team might make space for more female team members. A White female principal who chairs the selection team might want to pass the baton to a Black male member of the selection team who is willing, interested in, and compensated for recruiting Black male candidates. Identity and power intersect in these spaces and require our thoughtful interrogation before we even begin recruitment.

Recruitment Data

Once your selection team is as ready as possible, it's time for recruitment, which starts with a public commitment to diversifying the school and making it a safe and supportive space for people with marginalized **EDC4** identities. If you want to recruit equity-focused teachers, then make an equity-focused commitment that shows candidates what kind of school you want to be and that you're making serious efforts to move in that direction. Consider the following message that was sent to all staff and families in one school community:

> Madison Elementary is committed to creating an educational and nurturing environment that embraces diverse and unique learning styles. As part of this mission, we're working with you toward creating an equitable school community that seeks to not only meet the academic and social-emotional needs of our students but also ensure that the implementation of goals, priorities, and outcomes are done through a racial equity lens.

What message does this send to the school community? What do these two sentences convey about the direction in which the school wishes to move?

Importantly, think about what messages you are *not* sending about your school. One Black educator shared that she no longer travels for work after several experiences walking into spaces she expected to be diverse but were instead all-White. It was unnerving for her. For schools that are majority White, consider the messages on the front door, in the hallways and main office, in classrooms, and on the website. Are directions posted in multiple languages? If there are signs or flags that communicate a diverse and welcoming community, are such symbols supported in your school's everyday work?

During recruitment, most selection teams gather data about candidates in a shared spreadsheet. One key piece of data to include is a section for volunteered demographic data. Gathering that information—if **DP8** it's available and legal—will help you monitor inequitable practices throughout the selection process. For example, make sure you're not moving a disproportionate number of White candidates to the second round. When building a diverse staff, you want to know if you are attracting teachers from the community; teachers who share a background with the students in terms of race, ethnicity, income, or primary language; or individuals whose identities aren't as represented on staff.

Finally, the team must determine where they are recruiting from. Usually, we recruit teachers from within our existing network. However, be careful about exclusively relying on network connections, as they tend to reflect the demographics of the network itself, which is often a mostly White teaching force. Many schools develop partnerships with teacher-prep programs and institutions, such as local colleges and universities. Prioritize programs and institutions—like historically Black colleges and universities (HBCUs)—that work with more teachers of color.

Either way, building a diverse candidate pool is essential. One common misconception is that it is illegal to recruit candidates based on race. This is not the case. It is illegal to use race as a criterion to *hire* candidates, but it is not illegal to use race as a criterion to *recruit* a candidate pool. When considering race, the team needs to be consciously aware of this choice and not unknowingly swayed by their own biases.

Bias in the Selection Process

As the team shifts from recruitment to selection, it's important to watch out for bias. There is no such thing as bias-free hiring (Abawi, **EDC1** 2018), but there are a few practices teams can use to mitigate bias:

- Remove each candidate's name and home address from application materials.
- Remove names of candidates' education and prior organizations.

- Reduce the emphasis on certifications and credentials (e.g., don't use language such as "Bachelor's degree in _____ required" or "advanced degree preferred").
- Don't rely exclusively on documented or written experiences.
- Avoid nitpicking résumés and cover letters for spelling and grammar mistakes.
- Send candidates the interview questions a few days prior to the interview.
- Use performance tasks that show candidates' application of their skills.
- Avoid time-intensive performance tasks, especially if candidates are not compensated for their time.
- Make space for storytelling and verbal reflections on equity and diversity throughout the process.
- Ask someone who won't be involved in the interview and application review process to organize volunteered demographic information about each candidate.

Throughout, stay inquisitive. You're not just finding someone to fill a hole in your staff. You're looking for someone who helps complete the equity puzzle you and your staff are putting together. How does the candidate contribute to the puzzle? How do you know? What evidence have you gathered that shows you this aspect of who they are? How would this individual contribute to an equity-centered professional learning community? **EDC3**

Résumé and Performance Task Data

Most of the time, a school selection team's first contact with a teaching candidate is the résumé review and application process. Here, leaders should balance being both data-informed and data-neutral. There are many pieces of evidence on a résumé or an application that can inform—and bias—hiring decisions.

How your selection team reviews résumés and applications can set your hiring process up for success in diversifying staff and hiring antiracist educators, but know that these materials are just the starting point for building a diverse staff. It's often through the *actions* of teacher candidates that the team recognizes their passion and skills. After reviewing a résumé but before an interview, using short, targeted performance tasks is a great way to gather additional data from candidates that tell you a lot about their cultural competence and commitment to antiracism. Such tasks help candidates demonstrate their alignment to equity in their work, and they give those who might not have had formal opportunities the chance to show their potential. As with résumés, if you're reviewing multiple candidates' performance tasks, consider making them anonymous to reduce bias.

DP5

Here are some examples of performance tasks that could be completed verbally, in writing, or both:

- Talk us through a lesson you taught that focused on a topic connected to race, identity, or power. Share the lesson plan and/or teaching materials and model a few short portions of the lesson. *(This task allows candidates to highlight their commitment to culturally relevant pedagogy and can reveal how they engage in antiracist conversations with students.)*

- Describe how you'd build a lesson around a provided text (article, short story, or children's book). *(Intentionally choose a text for the candidate that has some element of identity or culture—possibly a story about an indigenous group of people or a personal narrative written from the perspective of someone with a physical difference. Candidates who ignore the identity and/or cultural elements will likely bring a colorblind lens to their work.)*

- Analyze a sample data set (either in a spreadsheet or as examples of student work) and make concrete recommendations for how you would follow up if you were the teacher. *(Make sure the data is disaggregated by race, gender, IEP status, ELL status, or some combination thereof. This task shows how the candidate would strategically redirect resources based on identity, and it illuminates their awareness of data and how they might contribute to building an equitable data culture.)*

Performance tasks, especially those explicit about equity, are an opportunity to show candidates what the school community values. They strengthen the school's public commitments and help show candidates seeking an antiracist school that they have come to the right place.

Interview Data

Most interviews unfortunately rely on our instincts about candidates' responses and body language. Those instincts are often laden with bias and shaped by our own individual experiences. We end up evaluating candidates on their ability to interview well—not on their aptitude for the position.

With this in mind, the selection team needs to decide what data and evidence they wish to gather and analyze from the interviews. Does the team want to understand each candidate's equity mindset and how they may contribute to a school culture working to dismantle inequities? Gathering data around a candidate's experiences and views on diversity and equity are important for building the school community you seek.

Selection teams that engage in any of the following exercises will take concrete steps toward reducing bias during the interview:

- Engage in interrater reliability. (See Figure 5.1.)
- Prime the team by reading an article about the value of teachers of color.
- Settle on a rubric the team will use. Watch out for simplified tools with language such as "0—Not a good fit, 1—Possibly and will need major support, 2—Yes and will need minor support, 3—A great fit." Avoid language such as *fit*, *good for*, or *qualified*. These terms open the door for unconscious bias to creep in, and they can reinforce existing power structures in the room. Indeed, clarifying objective criteria has been shown to result in more people of color getting job offers (Williams & Mihaylo, 2019).
- Be adaptable and ready to update outdated criteria. For instance, Andrew once hired a leader whose application had enough spelling and grammar errors that he nearly ruled her out. In the past, if he saw a grammatical error on a résumé or performance task, he'd assume the candidate was inattentive to details. However, he realized he was displaying a norm of White supremacy culture in the workplace when he chose to prioritize perfectionism and the written word. The leader he ultimately hired ended up being one of the strongest leaders with whom he worked, and her verbal communication skills and emotional intelligence made up for any writing-related gaps. As a Black woman who had attended schools that were not unlike the schools she would be leading, she brought

a wealth of expertise to the work that her written job application simply did not reflect.

FIGURE 5.1 • Interrater Reliability Process

Interrater reliability is used for norming scores across everyone responsible for scoring interviews, instruction, performance evaluations, or student work. The purpose of interrater reliability is to ensure that all raters are using an evaluative rubric or tool in a similar way and have a common understanding of the language used. This becomes even more important when making significant shifts (e.g., adding an equity lens) in what the team is looking for in a candidate.

The following steps are an example of one approach, but the process could be applied to other settings.

1. **Train:** Help new members of the team become familiarized with the interview scoring rubric.
2. **Observe:** As a team, watch a video of a sample interview, or have experienced selection team members model a mock interview. As the team observes, they should gather low-inference data on the responses, ideally scripting the applicant's responses.
3. **Score:** The team should be given ample time to *independently* score the applicant on the interview rubric. Emphasize the importance of gathering everyone's honest scores that are grounded in evidence.
4. **Collect scores:** Collect each evaluator's scores for the lesson simultaneously so nobody can see other answers and adjust their initial reactions based on them.
5. **Norm the discussion:** The most experienced evaluator should highlight areas of notable discrepancy. Depending on the available time, the team may only discuss a few of the indicators in detail, targeting those with the largest range of scores. Those will indicate areas of disagreement—and a need for norming. Whenever possible, the team should talk through each area and share specific evidence they gathered during the interview. Watch out for language such as "I feel like…" or "I loved how…" or "I wish they would have…" These phrases often preface inferential, reactive, or biased evidence.

DP3

EDC2

The questions you pose in the interview will determine the data you gather—and direct the selection team toward certain candidates over others. We recommend revisiting your list of interview questions and consider incorporating the following questions, which are designed to favor equity-focused candidates of color and White candidates with a passion for antiracism (Ryan, 2020):

Self-Awareness

- In what ways does your identity show up in your teaching?
- Tell us about a time when you did something inequitable or problematic as a teacher and how you handled the situation or how you would have handled the situation differently.

Working with Students
- What are some culturally competent pedagogical approaches you use on a daily basis?
- In what ways do you tap into students' background knowledge and lived experiences?
- Tell us about how you made a lesson you taught equitable.
- Tell us about how you demonstrated cultural competence in building a relationship with a student or family member.

Working with Colleagues
- Share a time when you changed your approach or style to better collaborate with a colleague.
- If you were the team leader for a grade or department and saw a pattern of racially inequitable outcomes on your team, what would you do?

Action Orientation
- What are a few specific ways you've promoted diversity, equity, and/or inclusion in the workplace?
- When was a time you responded to a student or colleague who said or did something insensitive? How did you handle the situation?

Scenarios are another key interview tool. We've heard a lot of White teachers with limited interest in social justice figure out how to talk about equity on the surface level. They might be comfortable using the word *equity* but often shy away from talking about race or racism. Ask a question such as, "How do you feel about working with students who don't share your race?" and you might get this answer: "I care about all students and am all about equity. I care about equity for students, and equity has always been an important part of my work as a teacher."

Consider instead sharing a scenario for the teacher to navigate in which you role-play a discussion with another colleague. Here are a few examples of scenario-based questions:

- In the staff lounge, you overhear a teacher of a different grade with whom you are friendly but not close to. The teacher is speaking about a student and says, "Jeremy is lazy and his parents don't care." How do you respond?

- You're three weeks into the school year. Stephanie is a proficient ELL student in your class who rarely speaks up and mostly sits by herself. Academically, she is an average student and has completed most assignments. Let's role-play a conversation you have with her at the end of class.
- *(Sensitive Content Warning)* In an all-staff meeting you are facilitating, an outspoken and influential teacher stands up and says, "We all know that those 3rd and 4th grade Black boys are running the school and need better discipline. They're acting like animals, and it's impossible for everyone else to learn." What additional information would you want to know, and how would you respond?

Making the Decision

As you start to settle on the final pool of candidates, go back and replace the identifying information and do whatever is possible to ensure your finalists include at least two candidates from a marginalized group. Research shows that the likelihood of hiring a person of color is 194 times greater when at least two of the finalists are people of color, no matter the size of the overall candidate pool (Johnson et al., 2016).

When possible, gather feedback data from candidates—both those who accept your offer and those who decline—about their experience. What drew them to your school? What did they think of the recruitment materials they saw? Where did they see the recruitment information? What did they think of the hiring timeline? Once you have this data, look for trends. What parts of the data were surprising? What does the data suggest you should be doing differently? Track your progress in addressing these trends.

When looking for candidates who embody a wide array of characteristics we haven't traditionally looked for in the past, our instincts may be wrong if we haven't explored them prior to the hiring process. Most people don't have an instinct for knowing if someone has done the work of interrogating the influences of their identity on their work as an educator. We don't instinctively know if someone embraces culturally affirming pedagogies. Therefore, we must make interviews more personalized. That's not to say a selection team should completely move to unstructured interviews. Research shows that individually scored, structured interviews are a good predictor of job success. However, many of the nuanced experiences and characteristics we are looking for in teacher candidates aren't familiar enough to us to build a reliable interview question.

Have candidates shadow committee members for part of a day. Get to know the candidates. Let them get to know the school community. Ask for feedback to understand what they value and how collaborative they are. Ask how they would address a challenge the school is currently facing. This personalized process can value the diversity of candidates and uncover experiences that might otherwise be overlooked. Once the equitable and personalized selection process is complete, the school should shift its efforts to teacher retention (see Figure 5.2).

FIGURE 5.2 • Five Practices for Retaining Teachers of Color

Although this chapter doesn't explicitly focus on teacher *retention*, school leaders have the power to create school environments that cultivate and keep great teachers of color. The *If You Listen, We Will Stay* report (Dixon et al., 2019) outlines various challenges teachers of color face and corresponding solutions, five of which land squarely in the hands of school leaders:

• Schools should be places that culturally affirm teachers of color (i.e., where the goals and values of the school match the goals and values of the teachers).
• Schools should be places that affirm teachers' humanity and racial identity, allowing teachers of color to feel free to be their authentic selves.
• Principals should create schools where they empower and invest in teachers (e.g., by providing pathways to leadership, informal and formal opportunities for mentorship, and the freedom to tailor teaching to the population of students in the classroom).
• School leaders should place a premium on building a schoolwide family where it's easy to build relationships, find a mentor, and hold one another accountable.
• District leaders need to make retaining teachers of color a priority by emphasizing methods of compensation for the extra work these teachers take on—along with prioritizing hiring and placement of teachers of color to build cohorts and reduce isolation.

These recommendations have many implications for the kinds of data school leaders gather about their staff and their thoughts on the school community—whether it's through periodic targeted staff focus groups or surveys that track teacher job satisfaction and feelings about the school culture.

Schools face a real challenge if they want to build a staff that can address the equity needs of their students and families. Making the teacher selection and evaluation processes more equitable is a critical prerequisite for improving the retention of teachers of color.

> **Apply:** *What is one change you could make to your school's recruitment and selection process right now or in the coming school year?*

Evaluating Evaluation

Once a teacher is hired and onboarded, their evaluation might be the most powerful source of data administrators gather and use—and this remains true for the rest of their career. Arguably, no single number in a school carries so much weight and has the ability to inspire or defeat. Students receive grades and feedback all year long on their performance, but teachers often see their evaluation scores only once or twice a year. As school leaders gather the data that matters, they **EDC2** should *deemphasize* the value of evaluation data.

Consider the following. What is the goal of teacher evaluations? Which of the following goals resonate with you most?

- To determine the quality of instruction in the school and which teachers need the most support.
- To ensure that every student has a high-quality teacher.
- To hold a high bar for teaching and learning in the school community.
- To help determine which teachers should be retained or let go.

Note that the first three options are about coaching, not evaluation. Evaluation is ultimately about the fourth option. Evaluation is a data tool for determining how resources—in the form of teaching staff—will **EDC4** be distributed equitably. (We'll dig into coaching more in Chapter 7.) In building an equitable data culture, school leaders should notice the necessary shift away from evaluation and toward coaching. In the remainder of this chapter, we outline why we need to deemphasize evaluation, and we provide recommendations for streamlining evaluative **DP9** data in service of equity.

We already know about the concerning rates of teacher attrition and turnover, especially among teachers of color. We know that teachers don't just randomly leave the profession; how much they feel supported by their administration (Carver-Thomas & Darling-Hammond, 2019) and how much autonomy they have (Barnum, 2016) are major predictors of teacher retention. We know that teachers of color must often navigate unfavorable working conditions and take on more responsibility than their peers, especially when it comes to supporting students with similar demographic backgrounds (Dixon et al., 2019). How does evaluation fit into teacher retention? We might hope that an evaluation system is a powerful tool for removing the worst teachers and keeping the best, but that's not the case.

In Atlanta Public Schools, a study found that just 3 percent of teacher dismissal cases mentioned pedagogy or classroom evaluations specifically (Saultz, 2018). We see a similar pattern across the country, where school districts dismiss less than 1 percent of teachers each year (Barnum, 2015)—almost exclusively for egregious conduct violations rather than performance. Evaluation systems don't typically remove ineffective teachers. Instead, they discourage and push out many talented teachers by creating a culture of micromanagement and distrust.

Andrew coached one promising social studies teacher who left the job because of her experience with evaluation. She planned culturally relevant lessons and projects, held high expectations for her students, and built strong relationships with students and their families. However, the school had a rigorous teacher evaluation structure that amplified an already demanding work environment. During a conversation toward the end of the school year, she shared that she was leaving the profession for good and going to law school.

"I'm tired of working my ass off and getting scores like 'proficient.' How can I be one of the best teachers in this school and not score 'atypically outstanding'?" she asked, citing the rarely achieved highest possible score on the evaluation rubric. As an ambitious high-performer, she felt demotivated when she failed to reach the top-tier evaluation rating year after year.

Do a quick mental audit of your school. How many teachers in the last few years have been fired or "evaluated out" because of instructional quality? Now compare that to the number of teachers who were fired for nonteaching reasons, such as attendance, insubordination, or last-in-first-out policies. Finally, consider the number of teachers who chose to leave but you wished had stayed. In our experience, and perhaps in yours as well, evaluation systems are a time-consuming effort that are rarely connected to the actual reasons we see teacher turnover.

> **Apply:** *What are your beliefs about the purpose of teacher evaluation?*

A System for Equitable Evaluation

Not every school or district can remake its teacher evaluation process overnight, and some already have robust, intractable systems in place. If that describes your context, then we encourage you to consider how you are prioritizing your evaluation energy and time.

We recommend a more equitable evaluation process and set of criteria that deemphasize the nuances of teaching and prioritize antiracist behaviors that combat White supremacy. Our evaluation framework helps us rethink how we manage staff in a school and foster a more antiracist staff culture. If you are a leader with an existing, less malleable evaluation system, you might ask yourself if these criteria are similar to those you use. You might use the following criteria as guiding questions or as a complementary layer to your current process.

We recommend using this evaluation process at two strategic checkpoints during the school year: (1) after the first marking period, or at a different logical stopping point relatively early in the year, and (2) about a month before decisions must be made about staffing for the upcoming school year. The first checkpoint is meant to address concerns or issues before they become habits. The second keeps the focus on the purpose of evaluation: to monitor staff performance in terms of retention.

At each checkpoint, teachers should complete a self-assessment, and managers should complete assessments of each teacher (using the form in Figure 5.3). Both sides add specific evidence and comments, particularly if the performance level is below "meets expectations." Although managers need to complete this for each teacher, which is time-consuming, this process is designed to take significantly *less* time than traditional teacher evaluations, which often require a 30- to 60-minute observation followed by 30–60 minutes of scoring and preparing feedback, along with a 20- to 40-minute teacher debrief. Our recom-

DP12 mended process takes half that time (or less).

Our framework is not a cure-all for the evaluation process or an automatic step toward equity, but it does offer an alternative approach to the data traditionally prioritized in schools. Centering elements of

FIGURE 5.3 • A System for Equitable Evaluation

Category	Performance Level *(meets expectations, improvement needed, not acceptable)*	Evidence
Equity Focus Centers equity and antiracism in their work.		
Relationships Builds strong and supportive relationships with students, families, and staff and reduces unhealthy conflict.		
Teamwork Cooperates well with colleagues, shares best practices, and seeks to learn and grow.		
Communication Communicates regularly and transparently, navigates healthy conflict, and openly shares and receives feedback.		
Teaching Actively teaches and engages students in appropriate grade-level content that aligns to standards and curricula.		
Essentials Complies with basic workplace expectations (e.g., attendance, paperwork) as described in the staff description of requirements.		
Qualitative Feedback and Recommended Areas for Continued Growth		

an antiracist school culture will help schools break away from default tendencies to perpetuate White supremacy culture. We believe this evaluation framework actually makes it *easier*—in terms of both time efficiency and prioritized criteria—to remove the worst teachers and create a sense of safety for the best teachers.

Note that we've removed any mention of *exceeds expectations*, *exemplary,* or *above and beyond* in this evaluation framework. Does this lower the bar? We don't believe so. We can celebrate the incredible above-and-beyond efforts of teachers while still remembering that a teacher's job is endless. There is always another parent to connect with, student assignment to grade and analyze, or lesson plan to differentiate. Although teachers can keep learning and growing—and we will certainly fight to make sure students have the best possible teachers working with them—leaders need to resist the temptation to expect near-perfection.

With so much trust and empowerment at the school level, evaluators have considerable autonomy with scoring. Consider this sliding scale:

pool of applicants – teacher attrition = intensity of evaluation

A lot of applicants and low attrition means you can afford a stringent evaluation process. Very few applicants and high attrition? Consider minimizing your evaluation system to match your context. If you can't find science teachers, then you might want to reduce the intensity of your evaluation of your current science teachers or else you'll be stuck with a long-term substitute or a recurring vacancy. Conversely, if you already have a dozen excellent math teachers who want to work in your school, then you could consider pushing out an underperforming math teacher through the evaluation process.

With this approach, we caution two things. First, teacher attrition is almost always a bad thing for schools. It's easy to think the grass is greener or that a new teacher with a bit more experience or a bit more passion will be better than the teacher who is struggling or who shows less investment in the work. Knowledge of the school context, including staff, curriculum, and students, though, is a superpower your current teachers have that most new hires will not. Second, you're not the only school that deserves to have good teachers. We don't need to create an atmosphere in which schools are fighting over the best teachers; we want our best teachers working with the most underserved students.

Every teacher you fire is a teacher who will likely be teaching kids somewhere else. As leaders, we have a broad responsibility to promote educational equity across our schools.

Conclusion: Finding and Fostering Racial Justice Companions

As you consider an equitable selection process, you must ultimately identify those people with whom you want to work in the fight for educational equity. These future collaborators will learn from you, teach you, and be your companions on the racial justice journey. As you examine your evaluation process, shift your focus toward collaboration and continuous improvement. A competitive, capitalist approach that pits teachers against one another for bonuses or accolades will ruin any semblance of collaboration in the building (Wiliam, 2018). It's time to move from a culture of accountability to a culture of learning.

6

Professional Learning Communities: An Extended Example of EDC

*Like all people, we perceive the version of reality
that our culture communicates… the coming together of two
self-consistent, but habitually incomparable, frames of
reference causes* un choque, *a cultural collision.*

—Gloria E. Anzaldúa, *Borderlands/La Frontera*

Javi's New Team

Javi has been promoted to 3rd grade math department lead at a large, diverse, public elementary school in the Midwest that serves 70 percent of students on free or reduced lunch and has a student population that is 45 percent Black, 20 percent Latinx, and 35 percent White. The principal and hiring team analyzed school culture data and determined that the school was lacking teachers of color in teacher leadership roles. Javi is one of only a few teachers of color—and the only male teacher of color—in the school.

Javi has already exhibited strengths as an informal leader among his colleagues. In his new role, he will lead a weekly team meeting composed of himself and two other 3rd grade math teachers, both of whom are White women. One of them, Jessica, is in her second year in the classroom and went through an alternative certification program. She has a lot of energy and enthusiasm but recently moved to the area and is still learning about the community. The other teacher is Linda, an experienced teacher who has been at the school for nearly 20 years.

She has a deep love for her students and the school, despite her frustration with the frequent new initiatives coming from the district and administration.

This chapter describes best practices for building an equitable data culture within the context of a professional learning community (PLC) or grade/content-focused team. We'll explore how Javi strives to build an equitable data culture, moving from team identity and mindset work to gathering and analyzing data that matters to making commitments in service of equity-driven change.

PLCs are spaces for cross-classroom data analysis—where complex challenges surface and are addressed. Researchers often describe PLCs as sites of fierce critical thinking and collective knowledge creation: "People in such a community are relentless in questioning the status quo, seeking new methods, testing those methods, and then reflecting on the results" (Dufour & Eaker, 1998, p. 25). In addition, PLCs are spaces "where educators can learn and unlearn whatever scrutiny, responsiveness, and strategic flexibility require" (McDonald, et al., 2013, p. 11).

Ideally, PLCs are places where teachers push one another's thinking, critically examine classroom inequities, and solve complex equity-focused challenges. The example of Javi's leadership, which carries throughout this chapter, breaks down some of the best practices and considerations for leading a team and creating an equitable data culture.

Step 1: Prepare Yourself and Your Team

In late August, Javi meets with his team for the first time. He knows the team will need to engage in identity work, examine the impact of systemic inequities on the team's teaching, and address implicit biases. He decides that the team's first meeting should focus on understanding one another and building a team culture. He begins with an activity based on *The 10 Lenses* by Mark Williams (2001). The lenses depict different ways we all view race and cultural differences in the world—from a "colorblind lens" to a "meritocratic lens" to an "elitist lens." Determining which of the lenses the team gravitates toward will hopefully help them understand how they see one another and their students.

Javi frames the meeting. Then each member reads a description of the lenses and identifies two lenses they bring to their work. Jessica shares first, describing how she often carries an elitist lens since both of her parents have PhDs and most of her childhood was spent in a wealthy, college-educated community.

"How do you think that influences your teaching?" Javi asks, probing to make a connection between her identity and her craft. Jessica shares that her vision for students is often one of attending the best colleges.

She explains, "That probably helps me keep my expectations of students high, but it also maybe doesn't make space for them to identify their own future pathways. I have to be careful I'm not imposing my own blanket definition of *success* on students." The conversation continues, with everyone sharing the implications of their lenses on both the team's dynamics and their teaching. Javi closes the meeting by asking the team how they felt about the meeting.

Linda shares, "I really liked this activity. I hadn't thought about how my assimilationist lens affects my work." Javi suggests that the team start to think about equity-focused goals in anticipation of their next PLC and mentions that he has another identity activity if they are interested.

After the meeting, Javi asks if they'd be willing to form a book club with the 4th and 5th grade math teachers. He suggests they begin with *The New Jim Crow* (Alexander, 2020) in order to understand systemic inequities and how they relate to their school community.

Here, Javi is engaging his team in explicit identity work. He helps them determine their purpose and reflect on the experiences that influence their worldviews. By facilitating conversations about his team's beliefs, values, and assumptions, he not only strengthens the team's connections with one another through vulnerable conversation but also sets them up to interrogate mindsets and biases during data analysis.

Doing introspective work as a team allows everyone to better support students, especially when the team's identities are vastly different from their students'. Most often, when we talk about designing instruction, we neglect to talk about the designers themselves. Many PLCs skip this step or opt for surface-level icebreakers.

Javi recognizes that as they prepare to gather and analyze data, the team cannot assume objectivity. They are influencing and influenced by what is observed (Hutchins, 1996). In order to understand their own subjectivity, Javi needs to help his team members reflect on their identities, understand systemic inequity, and integrate bias-reduction strategies.

Reflect on Identities

Javi models one approach to helping his team members reflect on their identities. Some argue that when we look at data, we "shift the discussion from irresolvable ideological dilemmas to a series of practical, pragmatic questions that can be targeted and addressed" (Bambrick-Santoyo, 2010, p. 61). This view suggests that data replaces subjectivity for objective truths. However, our identities and biases can't be separated from our data work. When we talk about designing "targeted" interventions, we often neglect to talk about the designers of those interventions—namely, educators.

There are many tools that help individuals and teams examine their identities and biases from multiple perspectives:

- **Social Identity Wheel** (Pabdoo, 2020): This activity provides an opportunity for team members to reflect on their social identities and how those identities present themselves and influence how they are perceived by other people. Understanding these relationships allows for greater depth of reflection with other tools.

- **Courageous Conversations Compass** (Singleton, 2015): The compass shows four ways we might respond to an experience, a discussion, or a concept related to race: believing, thinking, feeling, and acting. Ever wonder why someone isn't as passionate about something in the news as you are or why they're ready to march in the streets while you're still figuring things out? The compass can help generate conversations that help us understand one another's unique and fluid perspectives.

- **Racial Autobiography:** This activity encourages individuals to reflect on pivotal moments in their racial consciousness, such as their first memory of an encounter with race or an examination of the racial diversity of their schools and former teachers. Since these topics can generate strong emotions, leaders should ensure there is a foundation of trust among team members before asking them to share stories or excerpts from their writing.

• **The 10 Lenses** (Williams, 2001): As Javi modeled, team members can explore different lenses and share which ones they are drawn toward. Each lens comes with some problematic assumptions, and this activity is helpful for unearthing them in a safe space.

Understand Systemic Inequity

Both inside and outside the PLC space, Javi and his team need to build their awareness of systemic issues that influence their students and themselves. There is a bounty of resources about the forms of systemic oppression and inequity that plague U.S. society. As leaders work to make change not just in their schools but also on a more systemic level, the following list includes a few texts they might read and discuss. Although Javi has already read these books, part of his role as a leader is meeting his team where they are, which might necessitate more PLC time spent understanding systemic inequity:

• *Critical Race Theory* (Delgado & Stefancic, 2017)
• *Pedagogy of the Oppressed* (Freire, 1970)
• *Why Are All the Black Kids Sitting Together in the Cafeteria?* (Tatum, 2017)
• *Faces at the Bottom of the Well* (Bell, 2018)
• *The New Jim Crow* (Alexander, 2020)
• *Promises and Possibilities* (Wing, 2018)

Javi could also tap into Virtual Appendixes A and B (ascd.org/Equity InDataAppendix.pdf) with his team and help them process data that shows inequity, explanations for why inequity exists, and the difference between equity and inequity.

Integrate Bias-Reduction Strategies

Strong leaders make bias explicit so it can be addressed (Creswell & Poth, 2018). Research from the Kirwin Institute for the Study of Race and Ethnicity suggests that priming your team with positive representations of different groups can mitigate bias (Staats et al., 2017). For example, the team might read an article by a Latinx woman or look at pictures of successful Black leaders prior to reviewing writing samples by students who share similar identity markers. A PLC leader can explicitly tell the team that they carry biases into data analysis and that one simple research-based approach to counteract those biases is to read about, discuss, or highlight examples of a minoritized group that portray that group in a positive light.

Andrew coached one leader to preempt implicit bias by talking about the strengths of her teammates of color the day before she facilitated a PLC. Together, they anticipated moments where, based on her facilitation patterns in the past, she might be quick to correct, assume the worst, or take up too much speaking space. Heading off biases requires thoughtful preparation and intentionality, and they saw both this leader's relationship with her colleagues—and their contributions—grow because of her willingness to catch her own inequitable practices beforehand.

> **Apply:** *How much time has your team—PLC, leadership team, or other—spent on explicit identity work together?*

Step 2: Gather Data That Matters

 EDC2

In mid-October, as Javi prepares for his upcoming PLC meeting, he begins to be concerned that the data his team has been focused on isn't adequate. The problem is not an insufficient amount of data; as in most schools, the 3rd grade team is swimming in assessment data. Rather, the team has mostly just looked at assessment data so far, and assessments alone certainly haven't captured students' holistic experiences in their classrooms. Javi wants to slow down the work of the PLC and make sure they see their students more accurately and in a more equity-centered way. He also wants to better understand some of the classroom challenges his team has brought up. For example, they have noticed that across their classrooms, student participation and enthusiasm have dropped—in particular, students of color often appear bored and disinvested in the lessons.

In the meeting, Javi shares a list of qualitative data collection approaches, and together they brainstorm ways to include student voice as a different set of data to analyze. Ultimately, the team decides to engage in a series of focus groups with students over the following two weeks. A few times per week, each teacher invites two to three students to join them during lunch. The team formulates a list of students, prioritizing those they've noticed don't "fit in" or are often disengaged. The teachers know they'll only have about 15 minutes with the students, so they develop a set of just three questions

 DP4

 DP5

DP3

to ask—questions they believe will generate meaningful feedback they can analyze in an upcoming PLC meeting.

During the second half of their meeting, Javi asks the team to reflect on their mindsets about students and their families in the hopes of avoiding deficit thinking before starting focus groups. They revise their focus group questions and settle on the following:

- How do you feel about math class?
- Share a lesson or an activity in this class that you really enjoyed. What did you like about it?
- If you were the teacher, what would you do to make this class better?

"Sound teaching decisions require sound information" (Nitko, 2001, p. 3), but what does sound information mean when considering equity? It took almost two months for Javi to realize that his team needed a separate, intentionally gathered source of data beyond assessments. Data collection usually defaults to what we can easily access or what we've historically collected, such as standardized or district-mandated assessments. However, PLCs create a space to seek out what we don't already know and what is unfamiliar. Leaders can center the interests, attitudes, and values of the school community when choosing data and evidence. Although that might be more work on the front end, the quality of the data will generate more meaningful action. Data work becomes more efficient when its purpose is equity-based.

Collaborate with the School Community

Most PLCs exclusively consist of teachers, which can create a data echo chamber. Collaborating with other members of the school community—especially students and families—helps bring them "into the room" so teachers can hear their stories and truths. Javi's team decided that small focus groups would create an intimate space for students to share and would empower students to dictate the data the team would analyze. Here's the list of qualitative data sources Javi's team considered as they determined how to include other people and perspectives in their data-gathering process:

- Student/family surveys, empathy interviews, and focus groups.
- Student/family stories (written or verbal).

- Conversations with students about their goals, interests, strengths, and growth areas.
- Conversations with family members about their children's goals, interests, strengths, and growth areas.
- Conversations with previous or other current teachers through a gifted lens.
- Observations from special education teachers, school psychologists, speech therapists, ELL specialists, and instructional coaches.
- Observations of student interactions with peers outside the classroom.

> **Apply:** *How have these data sources formally or informally influenced your school? Which do you want to use more intentionally in your school's data conversations?*

Set an Equitable Purpose for Data Analysis

"What's expected must be inspected" is a common leadership adage that captures the importance of setting a clear purpose for data anlysis. If you want equitable outcomes, then you must look for equity. Javi's realization that they weren't getting enough actionable data from the assessment data was a key moment in shifting his team's work toward a more equitable purpose. Anecdotally, his team saw that students of color appeared less engaged. His team's goal was for students to learn, but student investment is a prerequisite for learning and an equally important metric to examine.

To set an equitable purpose, Javi's team needed to informally identify inequities or possible inequities. Through anecdotal teacher obser- **DP10** vation, the team hypothesized that their lessons or teaching styles might not be culturally competent for students of color. As the team continues to examine the data from the student focus groups, they will likely notice more evidence of inequities. They can then triangulate **DP8** their findings by looking at assessment data and disaggregating it by race.

Center the Experiences of Minoritized Groups

Javi's team ultimately used focus groups because they provide a clear avenue toward understanding the experiences of a specific group of individuals. Instead of holding focus groups for *all* students, they recognized that students of color seemed to be having a worse learning experience. Even if their focus groups yield different or conflicting results, their process is equity-focused. They are redistributing their time and energy to prioritize data that illuminates the experience of a historically disenfranchised population in the school.

Additionally, by making the focus groups optional, short, and during the school day, the team reduces the burden on students. Ideally, this data-gathering process does more than just provide more data to analyze. It also strengthens the relationships and trust between students and teachers, and it undoubtedly results in more culturally competent pedagogy and empathic interactions with students of color.

> **Apply:** *What data do teachers spend time analyzing in meetings? What data might be missing from those meetings?*

 EDC3 ## Step 3: Engage in Asset-Based Analysis

"Well, that was tough to hear," says Linda at the beginning of the team's next meeting.

"Yeah, our kids really opened up about a lot," Javi replies. "I'm excited to discuss the data, though. And since we're going to be analyzing some pretty intimate perspectives from students, I think we should start with some intention setting and agreements. We'll then use BITES."

The team discusses a few agreements about how they'll review the data, including "Stories and perspectives are real, valid, and powerful forms of data" and "Use data about students to better serve students." Then they each silently write an intention for how they'll show up, which they'll revisit at the end of the meeting.

With Javi's guidance, the team moves through each stage of BITES. They talk about the types of responses they'd like to hear from students, such as "I love math" or "This is my favorite class and I'm learning a lot." Although they don't necessarily expect responses like that from students, it's where they want their students to be at some point soon. The team then shares a few individual responses that stood out to them and discusses overall trends. During the (E) equity stage, Javi brings in intersectionality by noticing that female students of color had the most negative responses in his class.

During the S (Steps) stage, the team decides they want to stay inquisitive and spend more time on the focus group data in their next meeting before making any major commitments. In the meantime, they set next steps to gather additional data. Jessica mentions that there was one student with whom she hadn't been able to meet, and she wants to hear that student's perspective. Linda decides to follow up once more with one of the focus groups. Javi asks if he could join her and even lead the conversation.

"I'd love that!" Linda says. "I bet you'll have some great questions, and I wonder if students will share things with you they wouldn't share with just me there."

Finally, Javi encourages the team to name at least one small adjustment—grounded in the data—they'll each make to their teaching in the coming week. All three agree they want to shift the middle part of their lessons to include more group work instead of the typical teacher-run, "stand-and-deliver" approach.

Despite the agreements, intention setting, and structure, much of the meeting is intense. Team members remind one another of their lenses and identity work whenever a statement is made that feels steeped in preconceived notions about students. As they read and reflect on one piece of critical feedback that shows up across the classrooms, Linda gets defensive.

"I know the curriculum isn't the most engaging, but I think it's fine. And I'm not trying to get fired for changing things up. I think they need to just pay better attention."

Jessica pushes back. "I don't think we need to completely change everything about our curriculum, but I do think it's up to us to capture students' attention. If they aren't engaged, then that's on us for not being engaging enough."

Javi is impressed with Jessica for stepping up, but a moment later, he feels let down when Jessica shares that she thinks the solution is to make the work easier for kids: "Students said the work was too hard, and I think we need to meet them at their level."

Javi pauses the conversation so they can talk about rigor. Consequently, Linda recalls an article the group read about disparities in access to grade-level instruction for students of color (TNTP, 2018). After the meeting, Javi checks in with Linda and Jessica individually to make sure they are OK. He knows this work can be emotionally draining, and he wants his team to feel supported and recognize that data analysis is an important opportunity for them to strengthen their teaching.

It can be easy to get stuck, distracted, or overwhelmed when looking at data, especially when you uncover uncomfortable or problematic findings. However, with the right framing and structure, team leaders can make data analysis productive and enjoyable.

The goal of a PLC should be meaningful, equity-focused dialogue about data that helps develop a common understanding and create better solutions for real challenges. An effective facilitator should set up the conditions for meaningful equitable discourse, establish agreements and trust that help the team challenge and support one another, talk openly and vulnerably about student data, highlight the positive, and ask questions throughout the analysis.

Set Intentions and Agreements

Javi wants his team to see students through a gifted lens. Although they established agreements at the start of the year, they hadn't explicitly talked about the in-depth and high-risk conversations he wants to have. Facilitators can specifically use equity as a frame for intention setting. A leader might start a meeting by saying, "We're going to take the next minute to set intentions for today's meeting. I invite you to set an intention that connects to equity in some way. Take a moment to jot down your intention, and then we'll share with the group." One team member might set an intention to "prioritize student strengths," whereas another might intend to "leave with a plan for better supporting the Black female students in my class." Whatever the intentions, this focus helps give direction and purpose to the analysis, and it promotes a positive equity-centered mindset.

Once PLC members get to know one another on a deeper level, they can develop agreements for how they work together. Working agreements—or "collective commitments" (Kegan & Lahey, 2001)—help meetings run smoothly and establish a baseline for equity. These agreements should be co-constructed whenever possible to allow for traditionally marginalized voices on the team to be heard. Pay close attention to which voices are represented, and push for equity language in the final agreements, which not only create a working relationship among the group but also reveal the various needs on the team. Most teams set agreements by reviewing a list of possible options, selecting a few each person feels strongest about, and then working toward consensus on the four to six most important agreements.

Unfortunately, many agreements reinforce a status quo that is steeped in Whiteness. Just as data protocols can reduce free-flowing dialogue for the sake of time, agreements often overly value consensus building, which can diminish the influence of people of color if the meeting is a White-dominant space. However, Figure 6.1 shows how most agreements can be slightly shifted to make them more equitable.

FIGURE 6.1 • Making Team Agreements More Equitable

Common Agreements	Equity-Centered Agreements
Assume positive intentions.	Assume positive intentions and take responsibility for your words and actions.
Stick to the agenda.	Use the agenda and protocols as a guide.
Monitor airtime.	Listen to all voices, especially those that most reflect the students we serve.
Stay present and focused on the topic or task.	Keep students at the center of the meeting.
Start and end on time.	Accept nonclosure and recognize that some topics may need to be revisited.
Take an inquiry stance.	Take an inquiry stance and always ask, "How will this work for the most marginalized students?"
Make important decisions through consensus.	Prioritize marginalized voices in decision making.
Stick to the data and facts.	Data doesn't tell us everything. Stories and perspectives are real, valid, and powerful forms of data.
End meetings with something actionable.	Use data about students to better serve students.
Be real and honest.	Talk about students the way we talk about our own children. As we look at data, imagine that students and their families are with us in the room.

Establishing agreements helps prepare team members for rigorous data analysis and moves them closer to developing equity-centered solutions to everyday challenges. However, those agreements aren't always followed. There are five common "traps" that many teams fall into. You can read more about them in the brief section following this chapter, along with strategies for preventing those traps. You can also reference the powerful resources on our website for ways to respond to problematic statements.

> **Apply:** *What are your team's ground rules for talking about data?*

Pull Out Trends and Elevate Stories

Javi's team uses BITES both to pull out trends and to elevate the stories of individual students. The structure of the focus groups allows for more storytelling from students, as opposed to exclusively relying on assessments to paint a picture of student learning. To this end, teams can make sure they are prioritizing stories by asking themselves the following questions:

DP7

- Have we talked about outliers in the data?
- What are the quietest voices saying?
- If we were to transform our instruction to better serve the most marginalized students, what would that look like?
- What is the story behind this data point?
- What are some of the conflicting stories we're hearing from students about our classrooms?

DP8

Throughout the year, Javi's team might leverage data disaggregation and sorting to help pull out trends. Strategically sorting and filtering data can quickly reveal inequities. When a team disaggregates data to reveal specific identity markers such as race, gender, IEP status, or ELL status, they also reveal outcomes for groups of students and can call out disparities. This usually works best as a spreadsheet, but placing exit tickets into different piles can be just as effective. Quantitative data in spreadsheets should allow for rapid sorting and filtering so the team can compare the performance of students with IEPs to students without IEPs in multiple classrooms. They can also sort data to see the range of levels across one grade, revealing previously hidden disparities. This discovery can generate an essential conversation within a team about not only why outcomes are so varied but also who teachers need to prioritize supporting.

Stay Inquisitive

Because most changes in schools are implemented quickly, PLC members sometimes stop asking questions about the data too soon. Leaders naturally want to get to solutions because student learning is at stake, but this can put them in the position of moving to action before the analysis is finished. In those moments, biases creep in and teams default to innate lenses and comfort zones.

Javi's team realized that they needed more time to process the data and seek out additional data before finalizing next steps. Teams need to remain inquisitive and be brave—and patient—enough to ask deep equity-focused questions that can't be answered in one session, such as "How much are heteronormativity and ableism playing out in our curriculum?" or "How much does our pedagogy expect students to perform White middle-class norms?"

Leaders must always look for what's different in the data. What is it you didn't already come into the meeting knowing? What are you learning about your students, the school culture, and the community that challenges your current assumptions?

> **Apply:** *How much does deep thought work show up in your data work? How much do inquisitiveness and patience play in your data meetings?*

Step 4: Take Action for Sustained Equity **EDC4**

Javi and his team come together after a week, and the first half of their meeting looks a lot like the previous one: revisiting team agreements, setting intentions, and going through BITES with some of the new data. Halfway through, the team seems to have gotten as much out of the student focus group data as possible. Javi decides it's a good time to push for some concrete next steps.

"So what are the big takeaways from our analysis? What are the implications for our practice?" He starts with high-level questions, and the team discusses, agreeing that they need to revisit some of their curricular resources through an equity lens. They agree to focus on cultural relevance when they meet to plan their lessons. They also want to use some of the upcoming PLC meetings to coplan lessons that allow for more student-to-student interaction.

Javi probes, "Are there any steps we want to take that are classroom- or student-specific?" Jessica shares that she's going to follow up with her coach about improving her questioning. "I really want support with asking questions that will not only be aligned with grade-level standards but also be interesting and engaging to students."

Linda shares that she wants to spend more time working with and encouraging students of color who said they didn't like math. "I think adding more group work time to our lessons will help free me up to really invest my students in math."

Javi asks, "I wonder how we might share these plans with students?" He waits for a while, but his team looks lost. He then suggests, "I think I might make a slide that captures a few quotes from students and show it on Monday morning. I might say something like, 'I'm always trying to learn how to be a better teacher, and all of you are teaching me so much! In just the last two weeks, many of you shared that you wanted math to be fun and that you wanted to do more of the problems with your classmates. I think that's an absolutely brilliant idea. So, guess what? We're going to try something out. In the middle of almost every lesson, we're going to take some time to work together on a few math problems. Does anybody have a good idea for what we could call it?" Javi hopes that having students name the new initiative will remind them that it was their idea and help them feel more heard. (His students decided to call it Teamwork Time.)

Meaningful data analysis must result in meaningful action. Often, PLC leaders allocate just a few minutes at the end of a meeting to talk about next steps, which are rarely shared outside that group. In some cases, a team spends an entire meeting analyzing data and doesn't even talk about what they'll do differently. As leaders embed this step of EDC into their data culture, they must budget time and energy to help their team make and follow through on strong, public commitments.

Direct Resources Equitably

One key element of a team's action items is how they redistribute resources. Many teachers are hesitant to suggest that they will provide more help to a particular group of students, especially if the group is based on an identity such as race or gender. Teachers might feel like they are playing favorites or giving special treatment, but *equal* distribution isn't *equitable* distribution.

Linda's decision to focus more energy on students of color who said they didn't like math is one example of redistributing resources in service of educational equity. When Javi sets up his students for Teamwork Time, he might intentionally identify Black girls as leaders of the groups since he noticed they were the least engaged. After analyzing data, leaders must ask, "Are my energy and the school's resources going to the individuals and groups who need it most?"

Make Public Commitments

Once Javi's team determined the changes they would make, they shared their commitments with the school community. Jessica reached out to her coach, and Javi shared his next steps with students. Making commitments public opens us up for feedback and additional support. Jessica's coach will likely be excited to support her with rigorous questioning, and Javi's students will be more excited by Teamwork Time, given how he included them along the way.

Teachers and leaders create action steps all the time. Clear owners and timelines for tasks help ensure there is follow-through. For simple actions, teams might use a template such as the one in Figure 6.2.

FIGURE 6.2 • Action Step Tracker

Next Steps	Owner	Deadline	Status Updates

When there is no clear plan for who does what, certain individuals are more likely to be overburdened with work. For example, Black teachers are more likely to be assigned to support students with more challenging behaviors (Griffin & Tackie, 2016). Similarly, women are often passed over for the "glamour work" that would help them get promoted and are instead left with "office work," which can range from note taking to less visible administrative work (Williams & Multhaup, 2018). Writing out a clear plan for who does what makes it more obvious when the workload is uneven and can help the team redistribute tasks so everyone is contributing.

Persevere Through Challenges

It's easy for equity work to stop even after setting strong action steps. Javi's team might plan culturally relevant lessons for a few weeks and then get sidetracked or realize their lessons aren't landing right. Jessica's questioning might continue to yield blank stares from students. Teamwork Time might fizzle out after a few snow days and benchmark testing.

Equity work requires constant vigilance. Here are some approaches leaders can take to keep their teams on track:

- Revisit identity resources such as *The 10 Lenses* and the Courageous Conversations Compass.
- Publicly track and monitor progress on next steps as a means to "member-check" decisions.
- Get consensus on group next steps. Push for critical feedback and "hole poking" before moving forward.
- Make sure those responsible for individual next steps agree with them and believe those steps are a benefit.

DP12

Conclusion: There's No Formula

Through their PLC work, Javi and his team have become closer and more willing to have the critical dialogue necessary for dismantling the inequities in their own teaching practices and the culture of the school.

There is no formula for building a great team, and there's no perfect scope and sequence for running a series of high-impact PLCs. Meetings should not be restricted to predetermined activities or protocols week after week, month after month.

This work requires flexibility. All too often, schools mandate that the first PLC meeting of the month is about X and the second meeting is about Y, over and over, with minimal results because the team structure is not flexible enough to meet needs as they arise. These strict routines for meeting foci often ignore the needs of some team members and the school community. The ideal PLC structure gives teachers the latitude to critically examine their own practices and to co-construct something new as a team that they would not have conceived of on their own.

Data Meeting Traps

Alongside best practices are "worst practices"—traps that can derail a meeting or worsen problematic mindsets. The following sections detail five traps to look out for as you facilitate a PLC—along with ways to prevent each.

Trap 1: "Why are we doing this?"

Some teachers are understandably skeptical of a data analysis meeting, especially if it isn't clear why they are examining a particular set of student data. They may push back against the purpose of data analysis and try to derail the meeting. Sharing data that implicitly or explicitly reflects our own performance can be uncomfortable, so everyone needs reassurance that something useful will come from the meeting. Often, the purpose of data analysis is to "find the root cause" or "diagnose the problem," yet only highlighting negative data points means we leave out a wealth of positive data. Historically, we also make the experience of data analysis pretty miserable. Talking about how we are messing up sucks all the joy out of the room.

To prevent this trap, leaders can

- Provide answers to the following questions up front. Why are we looking at data? Why are we looking at *this* specific data? What are we looking for? Framing could sound like, "In the next 30 minutes, let's try to determine not just how students did on standard 5.1.A but also the specific ways we can address misconceptions in tomorrow's lesson."

- Include the team in decision making around the data you'll gather. Teachers won't ask *why* if they have already agreed to the decisions the team is making.
- Celebrate successes when reviewing data, especially if equity gaps are narrowed or closed. You might focus on what skills students were successful with on the most recent benchmark exam and revisit how you taught those lessons to pull out existing best practices from your team's toolbelt that are worth replicating.

Trap 2: "I forgot my data."

Many PLCs begin with the realization that only half the teachers brought in the student work the group agreed to pull together. This is usually a reflection of one of two things: either the team culture isn't ready for serious data analysis because there is not enough established vulnerability, or communication leading up to the meeting wasn't clear enough. Don't expect a team to be immediately open to sharing their data. Imagine a dean who is new to the school. If the first leadership team meeting of the year launches straight into analyzing climate data and potentially putting the dean on the defensive, the meeting is a risky one.

To prevent this trap, leaders can

- Share their own data—especially when it exposes a weakness—to make the process feel safer and boost vulnerability.
- Overcommunicate directions during and between meetings using email, text, and in-person reminders. A simple, nonthreatening phrase that might help is "A friendly reminder that..."
- Take an extra minute or two at the end of a PLC meeting to clarify what the next meeting will focus on. For example, "Next week, we'll look through Monday's math exit tickets, so please make sure you have yours ready."

Trap 3: "We're drowning in data."

Sometimes, there are piles of data and limited time to review it. Andrew observed one team bring more than 100 student essays to a 30-minute data analysis meeting. Not surprisingly, they felt frustrated because they were only able to "get through" a third of them and didn't have anything to show for their work. Gathering what matters must be balanced with finding the "just right" amount of data to review so PLC members can go deep enough into their analysis and take time to review individual student work.

To prevent this trap, leaders can

- Lean on electronic tools that can easily sort and filter large amounts of data.
- Assign a reasonable amount of data analysis as prework for the meeting. Often, asking teachers to score assessments on a rubric or grade assignments in advance can make for more meaningful conversations during the meeting.
- Facilitate group data analysis of one colleague's work. Trade student work samples or examine one another's data sets, which can translate into a heightened level of focus. Although those meetings put one teacher in the spotlight, the collaborative analysis counters that teacher's biases. Data analysis should not be an independent excursion.
- Use Virtual Appendix G (ascd.org/EquityInDataAppendix.pdf) when planning a meeting. Determine which layer makes the most sense based on the purpose of the meeting. The questions will help guide the conversation, and the "take action" section shows what the outcome might be for the meeting.

Trap 4: "I'm/They're the worst."

There are two thinking traps in the field of positive psychology that pop up frequently in data conversations. The first is to blame yourself: "Students failed the test because I'm a terrible teacher." This trap results in defeatist thinking. Although it speaks to the agency teachers have, it also overstates that agency and can be unproductive. The second trap is to blame someone else, often the students and their families: "I'm so disappointed with them. They didn't even try. And I don't think their parents care." This trap externalizes the blame and removes all responsibility from the teacher, which is also unproductive. The truth is that the answer often lies somewhere in the middle.

To prevent this trap, leaders can

- Catch themselves and their colleagues when the conversation might take a negative turn. Reframing or preempting "bad data" with inquisitiveness can help. For example, you might say, "I'm not happy with this data, but I'm really curious what I could do better next time."

- Before reviewing data, discuss both thinking traps. Ask team members which one they tend to default toward, and then have everyone write a sentence or two to themselves that will keep them positive and solutions-oriented once the data analysis begins.

Trap 5: "I don't see color."

Problematic comments such as "I don't see color" are not only rampant in society but also present in schools. Looking at data can unearth racist mindsets, especially as people try to distance themselves from the cause of disappointing academic results. PLC leaders can only spend so much time norming. Certainly, patterns among teams will emerge and facilitators can, over time, strategically frame meetings and design agreements to combat anticipated issues. However, leaders must also be equipped to manage emergent conflicts and problematic responses in the moment.

To prevent this trap, leaders can

- Draw on Virtual Appendix D (ascd.org/EquityInDataAppendix.pdf), which is a detailed list of commonly heard problematic comments and possible ways to respond to them. The responses are grounded in the work of Kathy Obear, cofounder of the Social Justice Training Institute.
- Role-play with colleagues and practice responding to problematic comments while keeping the team agreements in mind.
- Engage in identity work and deepen the team's understanding of systemic inequity.
- Use the 24-hour rule. If you can't find the words to respond in the moment, be sure to follow up with the person who made the problematic comments within 24 hours. This will help reduce the likelihood of future harm, and it prioritizes team healing before resentment grows.

7

Professional Learning:
Action Research and Coaching

*The world becomes more rewarding when you
let yourself look beyond what you're searching for.*

—Candy Chang (quoted in Bennett, 2019)

A First-Year Teacher's Journal

"Before I started teaching, someone told me I'd forget my first year in the classroom no matter what. I saw that as a challenge. I was determined to make sure my first year wasn't a blur and I was able to learn from it and remember important moments." Entering her first year in the classroom, 6th grade teacher Christy Chang had a brilliant idea. She would use a journal to capture the experiences and stories from what she knew would be a life-changing year.

Most days, she would set aside time with her teaching journal—sometimes just a few minutes, sometimes more—to sketch a moment from her day, map out a possible seating arrangement in her class, write something a student said, jot down glows and grows from her teaching that day, or paste in a particularly fascinating piece of student work. Christy loved to create, draw, and write, so her journaling time was something she looked forward to, and it became an essential routine for processing her work. Her journal was her therapy after a difficult interaction with a student, her to-do list when her mind was scattered during a busy stretch of the year, and her motivational speaker when she needed a win. Partway through the year, she showed her journal to her students and pitched them on the idea of starting their own journals. Students were immediately excited to have their own private space for process-ing and reflection. Talking with students about their mutual journal-ing experiences soon became a relationship-building tool on which Christy relied.

Little did she know, but Christy was engaging in a data collection best practice. Her journal had no lines, parameters, or structure she was required to follow. It was not a requirement. Instead, she reflected, "I felt like I had ownership. When I was asked to do something for compliance or to fill out a form, I never wanted to do it. There was no intrinsic motivation to do that, but the notebook was a structure that felt creative and that I started myself. It didn't have many constraints and was the way I felt most motivated to learn from my mistakes with-out getting burned out."

Christy's story highlights what is currently lacking in professional learning: the opportunity for teachers to lead their own learning and feel invested in and in charge of the data they encounter daily.

In many schools, professional development (PD) is a dreaded ele-ment in a teacher's week. We have observed teachers sit patiently through lengthy lectures about a new schoolwide initiative that comes with no guidance, next steps, or ongoing support plan. PD (including workshops, trainings, and coaching) too often center three concerning mindsets: teacher blaming, top-down control, and compliance.

The theoretical underpinning of most professional learning activities is that if we can just get teachers to do a better job, we'll solve edu-cation's problems. Though growth in teaching practices is absolutely important, placing all outcomes on teachers' shoulders ignores the sys-temic impediments they face. This mindset places an additional burden on teachers in low-income districts. The second problematic mindset is top-down control. Most professional development ideas stem from macrolevel data that paints a broad picture of what's taking place in classrooms. Teachers often have little input into what they learn, while administrators and district leaders dictate the PD agenda and learning pathways. Unfortunately, learning is often conflated with compliance. For instance, a district roll-out of a new technology platform might include teacher training in that program, but rarely does that training deepen teachers' instructional or pedagogical expertise in the long term.

By emphasizing professional learning instead of professional development, we can counter these three problematic mindsets. This chapter reimagines data use through two forms of professional learning: action research and individualized coaching. These two approaches to professional learning center three equity-oriented mindsets. The first mindset is inquiry-based. Instead of blaming teachers, an inquiry stance acknowledges that there is neither a single solution to educational inequity nor a single data point to utilize. The second mindset is collaboration. In place of top-down control, administrators and leaders see their role as a collaborator and support to the needs that teachers identify. The third mindset is problem-specific. As opposed to district or school compliance-based approaches, a problem-centered approach examines data that illuminate the individualized challenges playing out at the classroom level. Teachers, therefore, take ownership of their professional learning.

EDC3

EDC2

Education leaders need to adjust their orientation of professional learning. Adult learning theory and basic psychology have shown that teachers won't flourish if they are not personally invested, but leaders can work with them to guide them through difficult challenges. With the increased popularity of instructional coaches during the last two decades (Domina et al., 2015), schools have an incredible opportunity to center EDC in coaching. Action research, an often-underutilized approach to adult learning, is a unique and powerful pathway toward helping teachers create an equitable data culture in their classrooms.

Action Research: Studying Data to Center Equity

Because of misconceptions about what *data* means, educators have paid little attention to a powerful, differentiated form of professional learning: action research. Also called practitioner research, action research refers to research conducted by people in their own workplaces—as opposed to research conducted by external researchers. In schools, this approach provides a framework for teachers who wish to investigate their instructional practices and gain a deeper understanding about a particular facet of their work or their students. In action research, "the researcher initiates change based on a feeling that something needs to change to create a better human situation" (Bell et al.,

2004, para. 2). Action research's emphasis on leveraging experiential, humanizing data sets it apart from traditional top-down professional development and takes a more equitable approach.

Action research and EDC can be powerful partners in professional **EDC1** learning. Action research helps teachers examine how their own identities manifest in the classroom, gather data collaboratively to study **EDC2** student learning and experiences, interrogate their own learning as **EDC3** they explore possible changes in their practice, and navigate complex challenges. **EDC4**

Many school leaders see action research as too indirect and varied, when in fact it accomplishes the most ambitious aims of professional development: to provide individualized, inquiry-based, and data-focused learning opportunities that invest in educators and help them improve their craft.

There are a few criteria for action research (Falk & Blumenreich, 2005; Hubbard & Power, 2003; Watts, 1985):

- Have an "insider" perspective. Practitioners research their own work, pedagogy, behaviors, and classrooms/schools while keeping their identity and bias front and center.
- Mix theory and practice. Practitioners study equitable pedagogical and theoretical approaches and integrate them into their day-to-day work.
- Focus on a problem. Practitioners take a pragmatic stance as they examine practical, job-embedded inequities and challenges.
- Use systematic research. Practitioners' research is intentional and systematic, tapping into data principles and research methodology.

Action research involves identifying a dilemma or challenge, posing a question, intentionally gathering data through a variety of means, interpreting that data, and then making adjustments to your practice based on the findings. It's a cycle of inquiry that occurs at the individual level. Unlike traditional data collection and analysis, which focus on formative academic assessments, action research allows practitioners to explore inequitable practices outside, or in addition to, assessments. One teacher might study a need for control in a classroom by regularly surveying students and holding student focus groups to talk about power dynamics in the classroom. Another teacher might explore what happens when they encourage students to talk about their identities.

DP6 A third teacher might examine changes after testing out a classroom meditation routine. Notice these examples aren't easily investigated with formal content assessments as much as qualitative evidence. We argue that these aspects of schooling are just as important—if not more so—for building equity and antiracist practices in our schools.

Another form of action research, participatory action research (PAR), takes an even more equity-focused approach by including students directly in the process (Bell et al., 2004). Smith, Huppuch, and Van Deven (2011) describe one nonprofit's application of PAR to better understand female students' experiences with sexual harassment. They started by asking a group of girls to research a set of questions and bring their results back for group discussion. The researchers shared, "We didn't view it this way at the time, but in retrospect, the assignment was a sort of mini lesson on data collection in the form of a consciousness-raising session" (p. 26). The group then created a safe space to share. Both the adults and students found that the girls "saw the huge impact sexual harassment had on their education, self-esteem, and overall sense of safety as young women" (p. 26). Including the students in the research completely transformed the way the staff worked to combat sexual harassment.

Begin to engage in action research by choosing an issue connected to equity, ideally in collaboration with students. This is a great opportunity to collaborate with the school community and center "the student's point of view rather than... the teacher's own culture. Students are the informants in teacher research... and central to the role of informants is being an active collaborator in these research endeavors" (Hubbard
EDC2 & Power, 2003, p. 1).

EDC2 The next step is to create a research question that defines the purpose and scope for your research. In some cases, the question may be rooted in curiosity, such as "How can I improve access to grade-level texts for students who are reading below grade level?" In other cases, the question may be experimental: "What happens when I facilitate daily small groups for students who are reading below grade level?"

In her teacher journal, Christy asked, "How does a novice teacher develop a reflective practice?" Her observations were anecdotal, with different pages capturing what she was struggling with that day or in that moment. She shared, "I felt like everything was going wrong, so the teacher journal helped me tackle one thing at a time. And as I started taking on bite-sized challenges, they would evolve. I was able to study myself and see what was important to me as a novice teacher over the course of my first three years in the classroom, watching a gradual shift from focusing on classroom management to instruction." For some leaders, the idea of giving a teacher autonomy over defining their professional learning pathway might seem too aimless. It can be difficult to come to terms with a core principle of action research—namely, there is no one "right" piece of data for teachers to examine.

Strong action research questions often start with "How can I improve" or "What happens when" and specifically address a marginalized group or an issue connected to equity. For example, you might ask, "How can I improve the classroom discussion experience for students who most often disengage?" Administrators can also engage in practitioner research by asking questions such as "What happens when I stop by the classrooms of the new teachers in the school at the start of every day and share a positive message?" or "What happens when I have lunch once per month with identity-based staff affinity groups?" **DP12**

> **Apply:** *Take a moment to craft a few questions around a topic you'd like to explore in your work. You might focus on a persistent challenge, or you might focus on a possible approach you'd like to take. Either way, make sure your question focuses on addressing an inequity in the school. You might draw inspiration from some of the examples in Figure 7.1.*

Teachers and administrators can engage in either action research or participatory action research. Although it might feel time-consuming, the "quick fix" mindset does not produce meaningful professional learning or equitable results. The point of action research is that it is embedded in current practice by studying naturally occurring data sources and experiences close to the actual challenge. The inclusivity and collaboration inherent to action research, especially data analysis, not only builds capacity of the school community but also empowers them as interpreters of data and decision-makers around the lasting changes they wish to see in the classroom and school. A school leader's work is always better when done collaboratively because the load is shared, making the work easier.

FIGURE 7.1 • Sample Action Research Projects That Center Equity

Teacher Projects

- How does classroom cooperation influence students with IEPs?
- How can I strengthen the independent practice portion of my lesson for English language learners?
- How does my teaching change when I'm working with almost exclusively White students?
- What is the impact of small-group instruction on the Black boys in the class?
- What happens when I use morning meeting time to make space for students to talk about their identities?
- How do female students respond to peer mentoring? How does the classroom culture change?

Administrator Projects

- How can we create a stronger community in our school for LGBTQI+ youth?
- How does staff retention change when we create affinity spaces for teachers of color?
- What is the effect of starting a biliteracy program on the school community's perception of the Spanish language?
- What is the impact of schoolwide conversations about race?
- How can we better support families of students on free and reduced lunch?
- What happens to teacher morale when we train staff in restorative practices?

DP10 One avenue for collaboration is the use of critical friends—colleagues who can help push one another's thinking through questions and feedback—during PLCs or staff PD time. Teachers can come together in small groups to craft questions, process their projects, analyze data, and get feedback and recommendations. Since strong action research projects center equity, leaders may want to set up affinity spaces for teachers to process their work in a safer space. These spaces allow individuals to share their true selves and unique experiences as educators—and the lived effects of their identities in school. They also provide a peer

EDC4 network for when action research projects hit roadblocks.

School leaders can advocate for reforms to existing professional development that favor differentiated, equity-focused, and inquiry-based adult learning. Andrew led professional learning for a group of 30 high school teachers and saw an immediate spike in teacher engagement when he rolled out an action research professional learning series. He had been struggling to find a one-size-fits-all approach to professional learning for a group of teachers who had a huge range of contexts and needs, and it just wasn't working. When he switched the focus to action research, his work became easier overnight. Suddenly, he could spend more of his energy helping individual teachers and groups of teachers refine their research questions, identify outside research and resources to expand their knowledge, and analyze data they gathered with their students. Teachers began to rely on one another as critical friends, and Andrew was there to support when needed.

 DP10

Returning to this chapter's example, by using action research and collaborating with her students, Christy discovered that her teacher journal was a powerful artifact. It was a single piece of data composed of hundreds of smaller data points, all telling a unique and insightful story of her first year as a teacher. Unlike her students' assessment scores or her administration's evaluation ratings, Christy's journal painted a far more comprehensive picture of what had taken place in her classroom that year. She regularly revisited journal entries to see the shifts over time on her own emotional and intellectual journey. She could see how her teacher identity was formed and what skills and concepts she struggled with. In her words, "Data has a connotation of being anxiety-inducing for teachers, but I embraced it in a way normal data wasn't going to. I took ownership of it. We think that creativity and data don't go together, but that wasn't my experience."

There are many excellent resources on action research. We recommend starting with *The Art of Classroom Inquiry: A Handbook for Teacher-Researchers* (Hubbard & Power, 2003) and *The Power of Questions: A Guide to Teacher and Student Research* (Falk & Blumenreich, 2005). Additionally, Figure 7.2 provides guidance for how to get started with action research, and Figure 7.3 is a useful action research project template. In the next section, we'll examine how coaches can support teachers in their professional learning via action research.

Individualized Coaching: Conversations About Data to Center Equity

Many models of teacher coaching lean on a hyperstructured and efficiency-driven conversation framework. Some coaching organizations boast about their ability to execute five-minute coaching sessions, whereas others employ an overly predictable model of praising and prompting. Most coaching leaves little room for larger conversations about teacher identity or to explore teacher-identified needs (as discussed in Chapter 6). However, coaching, like other kinds of relationship building, is extremely personal. We each have our own styles, approaches, and techniques. Sure, there are best practices that can be applied across contexts, but we caution instructional coaches not to latch on to a single approach or framework.

FIGURE 7.2 • **How to Kickstart a Year of Action Research**

We recommend that school leaders "walk the walk" of action research by engaging in action research projects *before* expecting their staff to do so. Once you feel like you have a good handle on how action research works, you'll be more inspired to bring the work to teachers. It is important to make space for the work. The following timeline breaks down when and what to focus on when implementing a year of action research with the whole staff or a smaller team. Most schools should allocate about one hour of professional learning time and one hour of independent time per month on this work.

• **August–September** *(2–4 hours professional learning time + 1–3 hours independent time)*
– Introduce the concept of action research to your staff. Consider sharing your own action research work.
– Teachers reflect on data (don't forget the expansive definition of *data*) and work in small groups or grade teams to generate possible topics and accompanying questions.
– Teachers home in on an action research question and develop an action plan over the course of a month and with the support of their colleagues or other critical friends. This plan helps them solidify their research and share it with others.

• **September–October** *(1–2 hours professional learning time + 2–4 hours independent time)*
– Teachers gather and begin to analyze data about their question. They may make small adjustments to the question or plan as they uncover hidden inequities or hear feedback and ideas from students and colleagues.

• **October–April** *(1+ hour professional learning time + 1–2 hours independent time)*
– Teachers engage in an ongoing cycle of examining data and making adjustments to their practice.

• **April–June** *(1–3 hours professional learning time + 1–4 hours independent time)*
– Teachers reflect on their project and examine the outcomes.
– Teachers present their findings and takeaways to staff. For teachers who have particularly powerful projects or especially enjoyed the work, they might submit conference proposals to share their work more widely. School leaders can share conference opportunities and cover conference fees to incentivize teacher participation.

FIGURE 7.3 • Action Research Project Plan

Research Question
What are you going to research? What other questions fit under your research question?

Context and Purpose
Where did this question come from? What data—numerical, experiential, other—is driving your inquiry? Why is this question important? How will your exploration of this question improve educational equity?

 DP1

Data Plan
How will you collaboratively gather data? What kinds of data will you focus on? When and how will you analyze your data?

Additional Supports
What literature or learning will you explore alongside this project to deepen your understanding of systems and pedagogy? What specific supports will you need?

Another issue with many coaching approaches is the lack of explicit conversation about equity. Andrew's and Michael's coaching colleagues report having a hard time finding "entry points" into equity-focused discourse with coachees (aka "clients") unless the coachee either openly asks for support in that area or verbalizes a deeply problematic mindset. A top-down, administration-driven approach to coaching evades the purpose of coaching: to provide individualized and authentic support at the teacher and classroom level.

The best coaching is "classroom-up" coaching that centers the teacher's and students' identities and experiences along with a close examination of equity using data. Using EDC as a guide, high-impact coaching involves four key pieces: (1) identity work with the coachee, (2) coachee-driven support, (3) leveraging data as a "third point," and (4) turning learning into improvements to instructional practice. The third point helps the coach and coachee focus less on the back-and-forth between them and more on something else—often a resource or data.

A common piece of advice from couples therapy is "be curious, not furious." This same concept can be applied to each core component of coaching. Coaches must remain curious as they help their coachees explore their identities, name and unpack challenges in their work, and examine data.

EDC3

When looking at data with teachers, we find that simply having a conversation about inequities isn't always enough. In many cases, coaches must push, sometimes multiple times, to examine the details. Data that reveals inequity is always present but often obscured enough to create a collective unwillingness to go the extra mile required to find trends and individual stories.

EDC3

In the following extended examples, we break down two sample coaching conversations with one teacher. One of the teachers who inspired the example shared how she had become more open to others and less judgmental from coaching; when asked what caused this shift for her, she said, "Honestly, it was the conversation you and I had about the lenses and traps. You opened my eyes." In these conversations, you'll notice BITES, EDC, and equitable data principles surfacing throughout.

As you read these two coaching conversations, look for the progression of EDC. In the first, the coach, a White man, helps Sara, a White woman (an 8th grade ELA teacher), unpack how her identity shows up in her teaching—specifically as it relates to peer writing workshops. They work together to reconsider Sara's action research question and plan for data collection. In the second conversation, the coach and Sara collaboratively analyze student work and set public commitments for how she'll adjust her teaching.

First Conversation: Mindset and Purpose

Coach: Hey, Sara! How are you feeling today? Did you have a nice weekend?

Sara: I'm a little tired from today, but my weekend was nice. Jenny and I spent Saturday at the arboretum. We actually spent a lot of time talking about the lenses activity we did in our school affinity groups last week.

Coach: Glad to hear you got to enjoy the beautiful weather. And I'm very curious to hear your takeaways from the activity.

Sara: Yeah, I think I figured out the main lenses I use: colorblind, integrationist, and multiculturalist. But I kinda got stuck on the part about the traps I might fall into with those lenses, especially for the integrationist lens.

Coach: Can we zoom in on that one?

Sara: Sure.

Coach: Maybe you can start by telling me a bit more about your beliefs as they connect to the integrationist idea. **EDC1**

Sara: OK. Well, I think diversity is really important. Like, we shouldn't be segregated or separated based on race, so the more people of color and White people spend time in the same spaces, the more we learn from one another and the better things are for everyone.

Coach: Where does that belief come from for you? **EDC3**

Sara: I grew up in a really, really White part of Pennsylvania. Like, there were hardly any people of color in my school and neighborhood. It wasn't until I moved to the city to teach that I started being around people of color. I learned a lot from them, and it really opened my eyes.

Coach: Thanks so much for sharing about your beliefs and your experience, Sara. I'm wondering what implications your upbringing has had on your teaching. You also mentioned feeling stuck at the "traps" part of the activity. Anything you'd like to talk through?

Sara: The traps. That's where I'm lost. I'm not really sure how the integrationist idea could be problematic.

Coach: Can I share some possible ideas?

Sara: That would be great.

Coach: When I think about racial integration, I think about how a person of color might experience integration, especially forced integration. People are more likely to microaggress those who don't share their racial identity. Integrated spaces might mean more diversity of thought for White people, but they might represent a safety threat for people of color. I similarly think about gentrification. Gentrified neighborhoods tend to start with the idea of integration. But the mixing of low-income and high-income communities often has a negative impact on low-income communities who, over time, can't afford property taxes and are forced out of their neighborhoods. That doesn't mean that wealthy people and poor people shouldn't live in the same community, but without laws and systems to prevent the wealthy from taking over the community, integration will all too often do harm. *[pause]* I know that was a lot. Any reactions?

Sara: I'm just thinking about how, when my partner and I bought our house last year, we didn't think about any of this. I should probably research gentrification some more. OK, but what about in education?

Coach: Good call. Let's consider schools. Integrated schools are something that a lot of research points to as super-important in improving outcomes for all students. But I like to imagine a perfectly integrated school system. Imagine that our district perfectly reflected the racial breakdown of our community across every school. In Philadelphia, .02 percent of students are Native Hawaiian or Pacific Islander. That would mean that in a school of 500 students, there could only be one student who was Native Hawaiian or Pacific Islander. If you were that student and your friends who shared your same race weren't allowed to be at your school because of forced integration, how might you feel? By contrast, 45 percent of the city is White, so a White student would have more than 200 other White classmates.

EDC1

EDC3

Sara: I hadn't really thought of all of that.

Coach: Remember those two articles we read a few months ago about affinity groups?

Sara: Yeah.

Coach: I wonder if you could connect back to those articles and expand on our ideas a bit.

Sara: Let me think for a moment. *[pauses for about 30 seconds]* OK. So, I remember that article describing why it's important for both White people and people of color to have racially homogeneous spaces. I still think integration has its place, but I also see how sometimes there's more safety for people of color when they don't have to deal with White people.

Coach: Thanks for going down that path with me, Sara. As we shift into talking about your action research project, do you see any implications on your project from our conversation about the integrationist lens?

Sara: Oof. It's making me think about how I initially grouped students in class.

Coach: Can you say more about that?

Sara: This is embarrassing, but when I made my writing workshop groups, I wanted them to be racially diverse, so I split up the six Latinx kids and put one in each group. I'm regretting that decision now.

Coach: Thank you for naming your feelings. That's a really powerful reflection.

Sara: Should I change the groups up? I feel like I messed this up.

Coach: That's definitely an option, but let's stay curious for a bit longer. One question I wanted to ask you today was what data might be helpful for me to gather when I visit your classroom on Thursday. Any ideas?

Sara: Well, now I'm worried both about how my Latinx students feel being split up and also how that's affecting the quality of their writing.

Coach: What if you collect student essays and we look at them together next week? Then I'll focus on gathering data on how the Latinx students are experiencing the lesson.

Sara: That sounds good.

Second Conversation: Data Analysis

Coach: Hey, Sara! How are you feeling about looking at student essays today?

Sara: A little anxious.

Coach: Say more.

Sara: Oof, I guess we're diving right in, aren't we?

Coach: *[laughs]* I know we've only got about 30 minutes together today, but we can pump the brakes if you want.

Sara: No, that's OK. Just recalibrating from a long morning.

Coach: OK. Is that where the nerves are coming from?

EDC1

EDC3

Sara: Not really. More that I'm worried students didn't do well on the essays. It wasn't my best lesson.

Coach: Can we tap into that feeling and set some intentions before we start reviewing the essays?

Sara: Sure.

EDC3

Coach: So, your action research question is "What happens when I introduce peer writing workshops to 8th graders?" What intention do you want to set before we go through the data analysis process? You might consider something you'd like to focus on, an emotion or mindset you want to tap into, or something else.

Sara: I think my intention is going to be to try to look for the positives and not beat myself up too much.

Coach: Great! And my intention will be to help us drive our conversation toward something actionable—ideally something concrete you can do in the coming week to support your Latinx students, since we're focusing on them in this data analysis.

Sara: I like that. OK, I guess we should start with the bar from BITES?

Coach: Yep! Let's take a look at your exemplar response. Talk me through what specifically we're looking for in terms of mastery of this prompt.

[Sara and the coach discuss.]

Coach: OK. I just want to reiterate that we're not looking at grammar or spelling with this particular task, so let's be really careful not to let any of those types of errors cloud our judgment. We're

EDC2

EDC3

just focusing on the strength of the students' arguments and how they use at least two pieces of textual evidence to support those arguments.

[Sara and the coach discuss.]

Coach: OK. Let's shift to the I and T of BITES. How does seven minutes of independent review time sound? We'll look for individual needs and classwide trends and then share what we notice.

EDC3

[Sara and the coach discuss, referencing a table of student responses organized like Figure 7.4.]

Coach: I'm hearing that students' arguments were strong; 22 of 27 had a clear argument that answered the prompt. But half the students either didn't cite textual evidence or cited examples that didn't support their argument. You also noted that Katelyn's essay was almost at an exemplar level. Anything in terms of *E* [equity] that stands out?

Sara: I noticed that my students with IEPs, Tami and Jessica, only wrote a couple sentences. I know they can do more.

FIGURE 7.4 • Sample Data-Tracking Tool

 DP12

Student Name	Race/ Ethnicity	Gender	Constructed Response	Teacher's Analysis

Coach: OK, so let's set some specific next steps. How are you going to redirect resources to the students who need them most?

Sara: I'm going to follow up with Katelyn, who is the group leader of the Tigers. I'll see how she wants to share her skills with her group, with the goal of helping them strengthen their arguments. And I'll let Mr. Perelman know that Tami and Jessica might need an extra nudge to write more when he pulls small groups next week.

Coach: That sounds like a really solid plan. Want to text Mr. Perelman right now?

Sara: Yes, that way I won't forget.

Coach: *[30 seconds later]* Now let's plan out that minilesson for citing textual evidence.

[Sara and the coach plan the minilesson.]

Coach: With our remaining time, can I share some of the things I heard from checking in with your Latinx students when I visited?

 DP8

Sara: That would be great.

Coach: Before I drop into the agenda a few things they shared, what would you like them to say to the question "How was today? How are you liking writing workshop?"

DP5

Sara: Maybe something like, "I like my group and I'm getting better at writing"?

Coach: Sounds good. I'm going to drop into our agenda a couple of direct things they shared.

DP6

Sara: *[reads; see Figure 7.5]*

Coach: Any individual-level takeaways or trends you're noticing?

DP7

FIGURE 7.5 • Sample Student Data

Daniella: I don't understand why Teacher Sara made us do this writing workshop thing. But I like my group.

Jaime: Today was boring. I liked yesterday better. We got to talk about our ideas instead of silent writing time.

Eduardo: I hate writing.

Kayden: I liked it better when we got to sit by our friends.

Sara: Eduardo's response really surprises me. I thought he liked to write. I definitely should have been clearer about the *why* behind the writing workshop. Daniella likes her group. Kayden doesn't. I don't know. I'm lost. I feel like I can't win.

Coach: Let's tap into two things. First, let's hold onto our inquisitiveness; we're not going to understand everything with one set of data. And let's loop back to your intention: don't beat yourself up. We saw some noticeable progress from students in the writing samples, and both Daniella and Jaime had something positive to share about the writing work. It's OK to feel a little lost. I don't think we have anything super-definitive from these students. What do you feel like you want to learn or do next?

DP11

Sara: *[pauses for a while]* I think I should change my action research project. Is that an option?

Coach: It sounds like the data we analyzed together is making you want to strengthen your question. What do you want to change?

Sara: I want to focus more on how the Latinx students do with the writing workshop. And I definitely want to change up their groups.

Coach: How might you rephrase your question?

Sara: What about "How do Latinx students experience peer writing workshops?"

Coach: I love it. And I have one last push for you.

Sara: OK.

EDC4

Coach: Talk with them about your project. I think your students should know and might be able to help you as you try to better support their writing growth.

Sara: I like that idea. And maybe we can disaggregate the data next time to specifically look at the Latinx students' performance.

There are many coaching moves and nuances we didn't capture in these two conversations, but EDC encourages layers to the process that traditional, content-based coaching often leaves out. Note that early in the conversation, the coach activates a reflection on Sara's identities in order to help her deepen her awareness of how her upbringing and beliefs inform her work. During the discussion, the coach stays inquisitive, pushing for Sara to go deeper with her examination of her identity. The "Where does that come from?" prompt is a particularly common question used by therapists to help coachees explore the roots of their thoughts and beliefs. The coach later uses the phrase "Say more," which is a favorite line of ours to prompt deeper thinking. Although at points in the conversation the coach might feel frustrated by Sara's responses, these prompts help him stay curious, not furious.

When Sara gets stuck, the coach shares his perspective. Notice how necessary it is for the coach to have a strong understanding of his own identities and those of his coachee. The coach must be proficient at mitigating and responding to bias and problematic mindsets. The coach had to do a lot of work prior to these sessions in order to fill in some gaps for Sara on even a small facet of systemic inequity. The result is that the coach pushes Sara in the first conversation to be prepared to apply her identity and understanding of systems to the data work that comes later. In this example, the coach uses a direct style to explain systemic issues, but he might have gone a bit far with lecturing.

During data analysis, the coach uses BITES to analyze both the essays and the notes from his conversation with the students. The simplicity of BITES provides a shared language and structure for tackling data, whereas EDC and the data principles provide a larger framework the coach can use to embed equity into his coaching approach. Setting intentions and agreements up front helps the coach address Sara's negativity.

Throughout, the coach uses the principles of professional development: inquiry-based, collaboration, and problem-centered. The coach also implements the four elements of high-impact coaching: (1) identity work with the coachee, (2) coachee-driven support, (3) leveraging data as a "third point," and (4) turning learning into improvements to instructional practice.

> **Apply:** *If you coach teachers, how might EDC shift your approach?*

Conclusion: Respecting Teachers as Learners

The foundation of professional learning is trust. This includes trusting teachers to pursue their own professional learning goals. Teachers who can carve out their own pathways with the guidance and support of coaches and administrators will be more engaged and invested in their craft. School leaders must focus on inspiring and developing educators by tapping into educators' own love of learning.

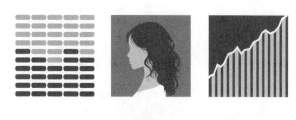

8

Conclusion

We desperately need an ethic of love to intervene
in our self-centered longing for change.

—bell hooks (1994)

Rethinking Special Education

Prior to her 13th year in the classroom, kindergarten teacher Nadia Baxter had not seriously considered how students with individualized education programs (IEPs) are often oppressed in schools, especially the underfunded school in which she had worked for nearly her entire career. Like many teachers, Nadia had limited training in special education and believed that IEPs came with a standard set of assumptions. For one, students would receive intensive services outside her class that would address their needs and close learning gaps. For another, her role would be to accommodate students' learning experiences in her class. Other than providing kids with more love, *special education* meant less: less capable, less talented, less work, less rigor.

Then Nadia started engaging in identity and mindset work with her coach. She examined her beliefs about students with IEPs and the expectations she was holding them to. She learned more about special education and systemic oppression. She compared her own experience as a mother of two young boys with what she saw playing out in her classroom. Gradually, Nadia started doing something she'd never done before: she expected as much, if not more, of her students who had IEPs.

After reviewing student data, researching best practices, and scrutinizing student IEPs and psychological evaluation reports, Nadia started to see hidden information. She saw that nearly all her students with IEPs were struggling; they were only a few months into kindergarten and already reading several months behind their classmates. However, she was surprised to see there were other students without IEPs who were struggling even more. She also discovered that some of the accommodations she had provided were both legally and pedagogically unnecessary; she didn't need to provide extra time or a reduced workload to all students with IEPs. She realized she had been helping students with their work instead of allowing them to work independently. For example, she found that when working with students with IEPs, she would offer more hints and do more of the thinking for them. Overall, an examination of the data showed that she had been limiting students' opportunities.

Nadia invited instructional assistants, administrators, and other teachers in the school into her data exploration. She kept the tone inquisitive and was cautious not to point fingers at others for her students' lack of progress. She collaborated with special education teachers to better understand data reports and discuss what she could do better in her classroom. She worked with an administrator to figure out new groups of students who would receive small-group interventions. She also talked more with families and paid closer attention to her students' affect during learning activities. Finally, she and her team dissected data in order to highlight students' strengths and identify specific skills to remediate.

As a result, her instructional practices changed. Instead of giving Carlos the six letters of his name to practice spelling, she added three more letters to his practice stack, just as she had been doing with the rest of the class. She saw the importance of Carlos getting access and exposure to the same level of rigor as his classmates. She started doing this for three other students with IEPs in her class and the two lowest-performing students who had yet to be evaluated. Lavonte met all his IEP goals within a few months, and Nadia was able to push him the same way she did the rest of her students. Lee was academically outperforming his classmates but had been struggling with the social-emotional part of kindergarten. Nadia began having restorative conversations with him every chance she had, even when he was having a good day. She held him to a higher standard by pushing him to process negative interactions with his classmates and helped him manage his social skills. Finally, she connected with the school psychologist to get two additional students evaluated for special education services, given that they were the furthest behind in the class.

Then Nadia took her advocacy a step further. She started requesting, then pushing, then demanding that the school provide additional supports for her students. With her grade team, she made a plan to provide small-group instruction and supports for students who were struggling. With administration, she fought to get IEPs updated, have additional services put in place for students, and expedite four required evaluations for a student. She helped her colleagues identify 12 students across the grade and set up additional small-group instruction plans for them with three support staff. As her advocacy spread throughout the school, similar shifts began to happen in other classrooms and grades. For example, another kindergarten teacher received the IEPs she had been waiting for, and the administration finally brought in a bilingual psychologist to evaluate a 1st grader.

By using the Framework for Equitable Data Culture as a tool for reflection, data analysis, and taking action, Nadia created a ripple effect that transformed her teaching, schoolwide practices, and outcomes for students. Nadia's story shows how any leader can help build an equitable data culture.

Stories and Transportation

We began every chapter with a story and wove other stories throughout the book because stories are an underutilized source of rich data in schools. We also included stories because they reduce negative biases. Research shows that humans who are immersed in a narrative evaluate the protagonist and their beliefs more favorably (Green & Brock, 2000). To the human mind, individual stories are simply more compelling than statistics (Bruner, 1987).

Hopefully, you're no longer a data scaredy cat, but even if you are, you might lean into the data around you that comes in the form of stories. We also encourage you to write your own story as it relates to equity. Everyone is going to engage differently with the content of this book based on their unique identities; continually revisiting your own lens will build your self-awareness and racial literacy. We all have a story to tell.

Apply: *To learn more about racial literacy and how to tell your story, check out Howard Stevenson's organization, Lion's Story, at https:// thelionsstory.org.*

Room Tone and Self-Care

The film industry uses a concept called "room tone." After shooting a scene, the production team records the room once the actors leave. Room tone is what an empty room sounds like. Most assume it's the same as silence, but every room has its own room tone, consisting of low-volume, subtle, often barely audible sounds. Room tone is essential for making scenes feel real and authentic.

Our charge as education leaders is to collaboratively seek out the room tone of our schools. Our surroundings constantly bombard us with data. Within that is the opportunity to create equity. We must audit—or listen to—what's happening, prioritizing the voices and experiences of the people we are called to serve. Remember, what's happening isn't always what we want to hear. You might discover that staff or students are disengaged or experiencing discrimination. You might find that the school has characteristics of White supremacy culture. You might find that students are experiencing more conflict in school than you'd realized.

It can be overwhelming to listen to the background noise of our schools—the things we typically ignore. School leaders carry the emotional weight of their team and often the whole school community. They carry data that reflects what looks good and what looks devastating. Listening and absorbing can take a toll on school leaders. Therefore, we need to check in on ourselves. We need to make space not just to listen but also to process. It can be exhausting to constantly be in tune with your school, so the best leaders must also set boundaries. You need to rest, both for yourself and as a form of resistance (Hersey, 2021). Even though this book doesn't focus on self-care, it is a call for us to slow down, reprioritize, and focus on the humanity of the people in a school building—and that includes the leaders.

> **Apply:** *If you want to learn more about self-care practices for leaders, we recommend taking a self-care self-assessment online and following the collaborative work of Veline Mojarro, Kausar Mohammed, Nadia Bui, and Andrea Manning.*

The Antiracism Investment

We want to be real with you about educational equity. The harsh truth is that the best and brightest school leaders don't have a magic wand or silver bullet. At best, schools can only partially compensate for deeply destructive systems such as poverty and systemic racism (Downey & Condron, 2016). We can make schools perfect, but there will still be factors outside the education system that create inequity.

Complete transformation and educational liberation require an incredible financial investment in antiracism. Ladson-Billings's use of the word *debt* in her term *education debt* is no coincidence. The average majority non-White school district receives $2,226 less per student than a White school district (Edbuild, n.d.). School districts that primarily serve students of color receive $23 billion less than districts serving primarily White students. Between 2005 and 2017, the U.S. government underfunded public schools by $580 billion (Alliance to Reclaim Our Schools, 2018).

Imagine what we could accomplish with large-scale changes to school finance and a true financial investment in antiracism. What if our school buildings looked more like Google's headquarters? What if teachers were paid like doctors and lawyers? There's evidence that even small raises in teacher salaries boost teacher retention (Carver-Thomas & Darling-Hammond, 2019). What if every school had double or triple the number of staff in every position?

We need a systemic overhaul of school funding, yet there is still so much you can do to move us all toward an equitable education system. At the personal level, you can learn about systemic issues, your own identity, and how to use data in service of equity. You can change your daily habits and behaviors, examine where you spend your money, and send your own children to the schools you are working to reform. At the interpersonal level, you can lean on empathy and trust as you coach and guide educators. You can use a gifted lens when you work with students and really, really listen to the most marginalized people in your school community. At the organizational level, you can center antiracism in your budget and public commitments. You can help your school redefine *data* as humanizing information. You can audit your school for White supremacy culture and interrogate your teacher hiring and evaluation practices. At the systems level, you can fight for reform in your school district and engage policymakers. You can publish a blog or become a board member. You can protest and vote for progressive policies. If you're not sure where to begin, check out Figure 8.1.

Investing our resources in antiracism is both a national fiscal responsibility and a local school leader's responsibility. If we want to achieve educational equity and liberation, we need to constantly ask ourselves where our time, money, and energy are directed.

> **Apply:** *If you want to learn more about funding antiracism, we recommend reading The Alliance to Reclaim Our Schools'* Confronting the Education Debt *(2018). If you want to fight for reparations, read Ta-Nehisi Coates's "The Case for Reparations" (2014). To get involved with the National Coalition of Blacks for Reparations in America (NCOBRA), visit https://ncobraonline.org. To get involved with the National African American Reparations Commission (NAARC), visit https://reparationscomm.org.*

A Call to Action

Beverly Tatum compares racism to a moving walkway at the airport. Standing still and doing nothing will still move racism forward. You can turn around and look backward and imagine antiracism somewhere off in the distance, but the pull of societal racism will still push you toward racism. Only when we walk in the opposite direction and resist that pull of racism can we engage in active antiracism and begin to see change (Tatum, 2017).

As a school leader, you likely discovered early on that it takes a village to lead a school. Families will fight alongside you in this work if you collaborate with them. Students will tell you exactly what they need if you make a safe space for their feedback. Teachers will log extra hours and take on leadership roles if you compensate them and they are invested in the school's mission. Antiracist work, equity-focused work, data work, and education transformation all require empowering the incredible humans around us to flourish and lead.

FIGURE 8.1 • Next Steps

What should I do next?

There are a few things we encourage you to do after reading this book, especially if you're looking for a place to start:

1. Have conversations with members of the school community about what data is, what feelings and emotions data brings up, and what folks believe about data. You might read some excerpts from this book to help stimulate discussion.
2. Adjust your data practices in at least one domain of your work, prioritizing an area that directly affects students, families, or teachers. Look back at your notes or a chapter that stretched your thinking or sparked an idea. Try something new.
3. Capture a larger set of data, such as through an equity audit. Lean on Chapter 2 for guidance, frameworks, and best practices.

What shouldn't I do?

There are a few ways this book could be misused or misinterpreted:

1. Don't think that this book contains an exhaustive list of best practices that will work anywhere and transform your school overnight. Context and community matter. Your expertise as a leader matters. This one book—just as with data—doesn't have all the answers.
2. Don't abandon quantitative data. Although this book highlights the often-overlooked value of qualitative data, that doesn't mean numbers aren't important. If you're thinking, "I don't need to worry about test scores as long as students are happy," then you've taken away the wrong message.

Apply: *If you want to learn more about teacher leadership, we recommend looking into Teach Plus at www.teachplus.org. Full disclosure, this is the organization where Michael and Andrew work.*

Seeking the Truth

Data represents a basic human desire to seek the truth. Our curiosity is normal; it's part of what makes us human. There is much we don't know, and the most ignorant among us are often the ones who believe they hold the truth. Collectively, data is just one tool of many that drives us closer to an understanding of how to make a more just and equitable future. Research and data analysis are formalized processes and systems for seeking out these truths.

Data can build awareness and generate cognitive dissonance. It can disrupt patterns in what we value or perceive to be the truth. It can make us say, as leadership coach Jovian Zayne expresses beautifully, "Something isn't what I thought it was. And I'm now completely uncomfortable with the former truth I thought I had" (Avila-Salmon, 2020).

Let's get completely uncomfortable, data scaredy cats and data warriors. We all still have a lot to learn about our schools and students. Each year, we work with new staff members, new students, and new families. Our communities are constantly changing. It is our ethical responsibility to seek out the data that matters in order to improve our education system. We can—and we *must*—use everything that humanizing information offers us to create equity in our schools.

References

Abawi, Z. E. (2018). *Troubling the teacher diversity gap: The perpetuation of whiteness through practices of bias free hiring in Ontario school boards* (dissertation). University of Toronto.

Aguilar, E. (2014). Setting intentions: A powerful tool to help us learn. *Edutopia*. www.edutopia.org/blog/setting-intentions-powerful-tool-help-us-learn-elena-aguilar

Alexander, M. (2020). *The new Jim Crow: Mass incarceration in the age of colorblindness*. New Press.

Alliance to Reclaim Our Schools. (2018). Confronting the education debt: We owe billions to Black, Brown, and low-income students and their schools. http://educationdebt.reclaimourschools.org/wp-content/uploads/2018/08/Confronting-the-Education-Debt_FullReport.pdf

Ames Community School District. (2017). *Tackling the racial disparity gap: Step one*. www.ames.k12.ia.us/2017/09/tackling-racial-disparity-gap-step-one

Ames Community School District. (2021). *Black Lives Matter at school week of action*. www.ames.k12.ia.us/wp-content/uploads/2021/03/Ames-CSD-Black-Lives-Matter-Summary-Oversight-Committee-March-9-2021.pdf

Anzaldúa, G. (1987). *Borderlands/La frontera: The new mestiza*. Aunt Lute Books.

Avila-Salmon, K. (2020). Why awareness is not enough with Barbara Furlow-Smiles & Sherice Torres. [podcast] In *From Woke to Work: The Anti-Racist Journey*. StudioPod Media.

Bambrick-Santoyo, P. (2010). *Driven by data: A practical guide to improve instruction*. Jossey-Bass.

Barnum, M. (2015). Fact-check: Just how many tenured teachers are fired each year anyway? (Hint: Not many). *The 74 Million*. www.the74million.org/article/fact-check-just-how-many-tenured-teachers-are-fired-each-year-anyway-hint-not-many

Barnum, M. (2016). Eleven things you might not know about teacher retention and turnover—but should. *The 74 Million*. www.the74million.org/article/eleven-things-you-might-not-know-about-teacher-retention-and-turnover-but-should

Bell, D. (2018). *Faces at the bottom of the well: The permanence of racism*. Basic Books.

Bell, J., Traynor, S., Stidham, L., Schubert, J., Kohrman, E., Hoots, C., & Cheney, G. (2004). Comparative similarities and differences between action research, participative research, and participatory action research. https://arlec-chino.org/ildottore/mwsd/group2final-comparison.html

Bennett, L. (2019). *Women amplified: 20 years of insights from trailblazing leaders from the stage of the Texas Conference for Women.* Greenleaf Book Group.

Biss, E. (2015, December 6). White debt. *New York Times.* www.nytimes.com/2015/12/06/magazine/white-debt.html

Bruner, J. S. (1987). *Actual minds, possible worlds.* Harvard University Press.

Capper, C. A., Young, M. D., Frattura, E., & Scanlan, M. (2020). The equity audit as the core of leading. In G. Theoharis (Ed.), *Leadership for increasingly diverse schools* (2nd ed., pp. 258–272). Routledge.

Carver-Thomas, D. (2018). *Diversifying the teaching profession: How to recruit and retain teachers of color.* Learning Policy Institute.

Carver-Thomas, D., & Darling-Hammond, L. (2019). The trouble with teacher turnover: How teacher attrition affects students and Schools. *Education Policy Analysis Archives, 27,* 36.

Centers for Disease Control and Prevention. (2020). About the CDC-Kaiser Ace Study. Author. www.cdc.gov/violenceprevention/aces/about.html

Civil Rights Data Collection. (n.d.). https://ocrdata.ed.gov

Civil Rights Data Collection. (2016). 2015–16 state and national estimations. https://ocrdata.ed.gov/estimations/2015-2016

Coates, T. (2014). The case for reparations. *The Atlantic.* www.theatlantic.com/magazine/archive/2014/06/the-case-for-reparations/361631

Crenshaw, K. (1989). Demarginalizing the intersection of race and sex: A Black feminist critique of antidiscrimination doctrine, feminist theory and anti-racist politics. *University of Chicago Legal Forum, 1989*(1).

Creswell, J. W., & Poth, C. N. (2018). *Qualitative inquiry and research design: Choosing among five approaches.* SAGE.

Delgado, R., & Stefancic, J., (2017). *Critical race theory: An introduction* (3rd ed.). New York University Press.

Digest of Education Statistics. (2021). Table 209.20. Number, highest degree, and years of teaching experience of teachers in public and private elementary and secondary schools, by selected teacher characteristics: Selected years, 1999–2000 through 2017–18. National Center for Education Statistics. https://nces.ed.gov/programs/digest/d20/tables/dt20_209.20.asp

Dixon, R. D., Griffin, A. R., & Teoh, M. B. (2019). *If you listen, we will stay: Why teachers of color leave and how to disrupt teacher turnover.* Education Trust & Teach Plus.

Domina, T., Lewis, R., Agarwal, P., & Hanselman, P. (2015). Professional sense-makers. *Educational Researcher, 44*(6), 359–364.

Downey, D. B., & Condron, D. J. (2016). Fifty years since the Coleman Report. *Sociology of Education, 89*(3), 207–220.

DuFour, R., & Eaker, R. (1998). *Professional learning communities at work best practices for enhancing student achievement.* Solution Tree.

EdBuild. (n.d.). Nonwhite school districts get $23 billion less than white districts despite serving the same number of students. *EdBuild.* https://edbuild.org/content/23-billion

Ewing, E. L. (2020, July 2). I'm a black scholar who studies race: Here's why I capitalize "White." Medium. https://zora.medium.com/im-a-black-scholar-who-studies-race-here-s-why-i-capitalize-white-f94883aa2dd3

Falk, B., & Blumenreich, M. (2005). *The power of questions: A guide to teacher and student research.* Heinemann.

Feagin, J. (2013) *The white racial frame: Centuries of racial framing and counter-framing*. Routledge.

Freire, P. (1970). *Pedagogy of the oppressed*. (M. B. Ramos, Trans.). Seabury Press.

Freire, P. (2005). *Teachers as cultural workers: Letters to those who dare teach*. Routledge.

Freire, P. (2014). *Pedagogy of the oppressed: 30th anniversary edition*. Bloomsbury Academic & Professional.

Ginwright, S. (2018). The future of healing: Shifting from trauma informed care to healing centered engagement. *Medium*. https://ginwright.medium.com/the-future-of-healing-shifting-from-trauma-informed-care-to-healing-centered-engagement-634f557ce69c

Goldhaber, D. (2016). In schools, teacher quality matters most. *Education Next*, *16*(2).

Green, M. C., & Brock, T. C. (2000). The role of transportation in the persuasiveness of public narratives. *Journal of Personality and Social Psychology*, *79*(5), 701–721.

Green, T. L. (2016). Community-based equity audits. *Educational Administration Quarterly*, *53*(1), 3–39.

Greig, J. (2018). Linking unconditional positive regard and teacher wellbeing. *Berry Street*. www.berrystreet.org.au/news/linking-unconditional-positive-regard-and-teacher-wellbeing

Griffin, A., & Tackie, H. (2016). *Through our eyes: Perspectives and reflections from Black teachers*. Education Trust.

Hansberry, L. (1984). *A raisin in the sun*. Concord Theatricals.

Harro, B. (2000). The cycle of liberation. In M. Adams, W. J. Blumenfeld, H. Hackman, M. L. Peters, X. Zúñiga, & C. Castaneda (Eds.), *Readings for diversity and social justice* (pp. 463–469). Routledge.

Hersey, T. (2021). How will you be useless to capitalism today? *The Nap Ministry*. https://thenapministry.wordpress.com/2021/08/03/how-will-you-be-useless-to-capitalism-today

hooks, b. (1994). *Outlaw culture: Resisting representations*. Taylor & Francis.

Hubbard, R. S., & Power, B. M. (2003). *The art of classroom inquiry: A handbook for teacher-researchers*. Heinemann.

Hussar, B., Zhang, J., Hein, S., Wang, K., Roberts, A., Cui, J., Smith, M., Bullock Mann, F., Barmer, A., & Dilig, R. (2020). *The condition of education 2020* (NCES 2020-144). U.S. Department of Education, National Center for Education Statistics.

Hutchins, C. L. (1996). *Systemic thinking: Solving complex problems*. Professional Development Systems.

Johnson, S. K., Hekman, D. R., & Chan, E. T. (2016). If there's only one woman in your candidate pool, there's statistically no chance she'll be hired. *Harvard Business Review*. https://hbr.org/2016/04/if-theres-only-one-woman-in-your-candidate-pool-theres-statistically-no-chance-shell-be-hired

Kegan, R., & Lahey, L. (2001). The real reason people won't change. *Harvard Business Review*. https://hbr.org/2001/11/the-real-reason-people-wont-change

Kendi, I. X. (2019). *How to be an antiracist*. One World.

Kuypers, L. M. (2019). *The zones of regulation: A curriculum designed to foster self-regulation and emotional control*. Langara College.

Lorde, A. (1984). *Sister outsider: Essays and speeches*. Crossing Press.

McDonald, J. P., Mohr, N., Dichter, A., & McDonald, E. C. (2013). *The power of protocols: An educator's guide to better practice*. Hawker Brownlow.

Motamedi, J. G., & Stevens, D. (2018). Human resources practices for recruiting, selecting, and retaining teachers of color. *REL Northwest.* https://ies.ed.gov/ncee/edlabs/regions/northwest/pdf/human-resources-practices.pdf

Nitko, A. J. (2001). *Educational assessment of students.* Merrill-Prentice Hall.

Office for Human Research Protections. (2018). The Belmont report: Ethical principles and guidelines for the protection of human subjects of research .www.hhs.gov/ohrp/regulations-and-policy/belmont-report/read-the-belmont-report/index.html

Okun, T. (2006). *From White racist to White anti-racist: The life-long journey.* www.dismantlingracism.org/uploads/4/3/5/7/43579015/white_identity_ladder_2013.pdf

Okun, T. (2021) *White supremacy culture—Still here.* https://drive.google.com/file/d/1XR_7M_9qa64zZ00_JyFVTAjmjVU-uSz8/view

Pabdoo. (2020). *The social identity wheel. Inclusive Teaching at U-M.* https://sites.lsa.umich.edu/inclusive-teaching/social-identity-wheel

Plaid, A., & MacDonald-Dennis, C. (2021). 'BIPOC' isn't doing what you think it's doing: Opinion. *Newsweek.* www.newsweek.com/bipoc-isnt-doing-what-you-think-its-doing-opinion-1582494

Plank, L. (2019). *For the love of men: From toxic to a more mindful masculinity.* St. Martin's Press.

Potapchuk, M. (2021). *Transforming organizational culture assessment tool.* http://www.mpassociates.us/uploads/3/7/1/0/37103967/transformingorganizationalcultureassessmenttool_mpassociates__final_4.21.pdf

Project Implicit. (2011). Take a test. https://implicit.harvard.edu/implicit/take-atest.html

Reardon, S. F., & Fahle, E. M. (2017). State of the union: 2017. *Stanford Center on Poverty & Inequality.* https://inequality.stanford.edu/publications/media/details/state-union-2017-education

Ryan, R. (2020). Black lives matter! Time employers update their interview questions. *Forbes.* www.forbes.com/sites/robinryan/2020/08/11/black-lives-matter-time-employers-update-their-interview-questions/?sh=44618fcc5567

Safir, S., & Dugan, J. (2021) *Street data: A next-generation model for equity, pedagogy, and school transformation.* Corwin.

Saultz, A. (2018). *What does one do to get fired around here? An analysis of teacher dismissals in Georgia.* American Enterprise Institute.

Singleton, G. E. (2015). *Courageous conversations about race: A field guide for achieving equity in Schools.* Corwin.

Skrla, L., McKenzie, K. B., & Scheurich, J. J. (2009). *Using equity audits to create equitable and excellent schools.* Corwin.

Smith, J., Huppuch, M., & Deven, M. V. (2011). *Hey, shorty! A guide to combating sexual harassment and violence in schools and on the streets.* Feminist Press at the City University of New York.

Staats, C., Capatosto, K., Tenney, L., & Mamo, S. (2017). *2017 State of the science: Implicit bias review.* Kirwan Institute.

Stout, C. & Wilburn, T. (2022) *CRT map: Efforts to restrict teaching racism and bias have multiplied across the U.S.* Chalkbeat. www.chalkbeat.org/22525983/map-critical-race-theory-legislation-teaching-racism

Strauss, V. (2015, April 28). Black male teachers: There aren't enough of them. *Washington Post.* www.washingtonpost.com/news/answer-sheet/wp/2015/04/28/black-male-teachers-there-arent-enough-of-them

Talley, H. L. (2019). White women doing white supremacy in nonprofit culture. Equity in the Center. https://equityinthecenter.org/white-women-doing-white-supremacy-in-nonprofit-culture

Tatum, B. (2017). *Why are all the black kids sitting together in the cafeteria?* (Revised ed.). Basic Books.

TNTP. (2018). *The opportunity myth: What students can show us about how school is letting them down—and how to fix it.* https://tntp.org/assets/documents/TNTP_The-Opportunity-Myth_Web.pdf

Wachtel, T. (2016). Defining restorative. *IIRP Graduate School.* www.iirp.edu/restorative-practices/defining-restorative

Watts, H. (1985). When teachers are researchers, teaching improves. *Journal of Staff Development, 6*(2), 118–127.

Whites for Racial Equity. (2022). Racial autobiography. http://whitesforracialequity.org/1-awareness-activity-reflection-questions

Wiliam, D. (2018). *Creating the schools our children need: Why what we're doing now won't help much (and what we can do instead).* Learning Sciences International.

Williams, J. C., & Mihaylo, S. (2019). How the best bosses interrupt bias on their teams. *Harvard Business Review.* https://hbr.org/2019/11/how-the-best-bosses-interrupt-bias-on-their-teams?ab=hero-main-text

Williams, J. C., & Multhaup, M. (2018). For women and minorities to get ahead, managers must assign work fairly. *Harvard Business Review.* https://hbr.org/2018/03/for-women-and-minorities-to-get-ahead-managers-must-assign-work-fairly

Williams, M. A. (2001). *The 10 lenses: Your guide to living and working in a multicultural world.* Capital Books.

Wing, K. J. (2018). *Promises and possibilities: Dismantling the school-to-prison pipeline.* Createspace Independent Publishing Platform.

Yang, N. (2020). Editor's note: Why we now capitalize Black but continue to lowercase white. MPR News. www.mprnews.org/story/2020/08/10/editors-note-why-we-now-capitalize-black-but-continue-to-lowercase-white

Index

The letter *f* following a page locator denotes a figure.

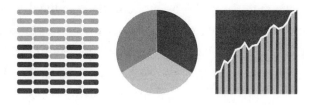

About the Authors

Andrew Knips (he/him) has more than a decade of experience teaching students, leading teams, and coaching leaders in Philadelphia's public, alternative, and charter schools. He is an education leadership coach, executive coach, data consultant, and racial literacy trainer. Previously, he was a high school English teacher and school administrator. Andrew has observed thousands of teacher team and leadership team meetings, facilitated hundreds of professional learning sessions, coached hundreds of educators, and collaborated on equity audits in over a dozen schools and organizations. He has designed dozens of data tools and systems for teachers and leaders. Andrew has a BA in political science, international studies, and Latin American studies from the University of Wisconsin–Madison, an MSEd in urban education from the University of Pennsylvania, and a K–12 principal certification from Temple University. He has presented at conferences such as AERA and NCTE and has published articles on blogs such as *Edutopia* and *Education Post*. He can be reached at andrew.knips@gmail.com.

Sonya Lopez (she/her) is currently a school-based social worker in Philadelphia. She has worked for more than a decade in schools in a number of roles, including language arts and literature teacher, school administrator, and director of social-emotional learning at a K–12 charter school. Across settings, her approach to practice supports a contextual understanding of individual experiences through a systems lens and a holistic perspective of identity. Throughout her career, Sonya has collaborated with clinicians, therapists, creatives, educators, and families in Philadelphia to shape environments informed by understanding mental health, resilience, sociopolitical contexts, trauma, and grief. She holds a BA in English literature from Villanova University, an MSEd in education, and an MSW with a clinical concentration from the University of Pennsylvania. She can be reached at sonyalopez02@gmail.com.

Michael Savoy (he/him) has 25 years of educational experience, including teaching mathematics at the middle school, high school, and college levels; working with community organizations on school policy, advocacy, and involvement; and working with K–12 teachers, teacher leaders, and administrators to improve the equitable education experiences and opportunities for all their students. Throughout his educational career, he has continued to focus on ways to dismantle educational inequities, improve educational environments, and involve more parent and community members in the success of all students. He is the author of several journal articles and book chapters on educational change. Michael earned his bachelor's degree in aerospace engineering from the University of Maryland, his master's degree in mathematics education from Salisbury University, and his PhD in instructional systems design from Pennsylvania State University. He can be reached at msavoyphd@gmail.com.

Kendall LaParo (she/her) is an education researcher and sociologist who studies inequality in school systems. She currently works as a quantitative researcher at Research for Action, an education research firm in Philadelphia. She also cofacilitates Philadelphia's Data & Assessment Community of Practice, a gathering space for education leaders. Kendall began her career as an elementary school teacher in Camden, New Jersey. While teaching, she discovered a passion for education research and now uses her experience as an educator to inform her data science work. She served as director of analytics at the education nonprofit Springboard Collaborative, where she managed data collection and analysis for three national out-of-school-time literacy programs that served more than 5,000 students each year. She also worked as a researcher at the School District of Philadelphia and Temple University's Public Policy Lab. She holds an MS in urban education from the University of Pennsylvania and a PhD in sociology from Temple University. She can be reached at kendall.laparo@gmail.com.

Related ASCD Resources: Equity in Data

At the time of publication, the following resources were available (ASCD stock numbers in parentheses).

The Data-Driven Classroom: How do I use student data to improve my instruction? (ASCD Arias) by Craig A. Mertler (#SF114082)

Excellence Through Equity: Five Principles of Courageous Leadership to Guide Achievement for Every Student by Alan M. Blankstein, Pedro Noguera, & Lorena Kelly (#116070)

How to Make Decisions with Different Kinds of Student Assessment Data by Susan M. Brookhart (#116003)

How Teachers Can Turn Data into Action by Daniel R. Venables (#114007)

Measuring What We Do in Schools: How to Know If What We Are Doing Is Making a Difference by Victoria L. Bernhardt (#117021)

Turning High-Poverty Schools into High-Performing Schools, 2nd Edition by William H. Parrett & Kathleen M. Budge (#120031)

Using Data for Equity in the Classroom (Quick Reference Guide) by Amanda Datnow & Vicki Park (#QRG119076)

Using Data to Focus Instructional Improvement by Cheryl James-Ward, Douglas Fisher, Nancy Frey, & Diane Lapp (#113003)

For up-to-date information about ASCD resources, go to **www.ascd.org.** You can search the complete archives of *Educational Leadership* at **www.ascd.org/el.** To contact us, send an email to member@ascd.org or call 1-800-933-2723 or 703-578-9600.

WHOLE CHILD
TENETS

1 **HEALTHY**
Each student enters school healthy and learns about and practices a healthy lifestyle.

2 **SAFE**
Each student learns in an environment that is physically and emotionally safe for students and adults.

3 **ENGAGED**
Each student is actively engaged in learning and is connected to the school and broader community.

4 **SUPPORTED**
Each student has access to personalized learning and is supported by qualified, caring adults.

5 **CHALLENGED**
Each student is challenged academically and prepared for success in college or further study and for employment and participation in a global environment.

THE WHOLE CHILD

The ASCD Whole Child approach is an effort to transition from a focus on narrowly defined academic achievement to one that promotes the long-term development and success of all children. Through this approach, ASCD supports educators, families, community members, and policymakers as they move from a vision about educating the whole child to sustainable, collaborative actions.

Equity in Data relates to the **engaged** and **supported** tenets. *For more about the ASCD Whole Child approach, visit* **www.ascd.org/wholechild.**